Racism and Human Survival

CO-AYM-155

UNIVERSITY OF WINNIPEG
LIBRARY DISCARDED
515 Portage Avenue
Winnipeg, Manitoba R3B 2E9

DISCARDED

WINNIPEG
LIBRARY

515 Portage Avenue
Winnipeg, Manitoba R3B 2E9

INTERNATIONAL PUBLISHERS
381 Park Avenue South NEW YORK, N.Y. 10016

Racism and Human Survival
by Claude M. Lightfoot

BY THE AUTHOR

Ghetto Rebellion to Black Liberation
Black America and the World Revolution

PAMPHLETS

An American Looks at Russia
Not Guilty
The 1956 Elections
Turning Point in Freedom Road
Building a Negro and White Alliance for Progress
Black Power and Liberation
The Civil War and Black Liberation Today

DD
261
.4
.L47

RACISM
and
HUMAN SURVIVAL

Lessons of Nazi Germany
for Today's World

by Claude M. Lightfoot

International Publishers
New York

To Carole

ISBN 0-7178-0364-3

Copyright © Claude M. Lightfoot 1972
Cover Design by Lothar Reher
Printed by Völkerfreundschaft Dresden
German Democratic Republic

CONTENTS

INTRODUCTION

The most destructive war in history was justified by Hitler on the theory that the Germans constituted the master race. This theory was rooted in the idea that biologically inherited characteristics are the chief determinant of superiority and that environment has little to do with contrasts between races. It originated in the works of Gobineau. The German people in Hitler's time were fed on a steady diet of racial, innate superiority.

These and similar ideas have no foundation in the natural sciences. On the contrary: Since the latter part of the nineteenth century, science has proven beyond a shadow of a doubt that biological differences among peoples, such as skin color, shape of the skull, blood type, etc., have nothing to do with the question of superiority or inferiority among peoples.

L. C. Dunn, Professor of Zoology at Columbia University, in a paper dealing with "Race and Biology" at a symposium under the auspices of UNESCO, wrote:

> "It was the first half of the twentieth century that witnessed the rise of the science of genetics, responsible for a radical change in the way in which race and race differences in man are to be regarded."

"The judgment of biology in this case is clear and unequivocal. The modern view of race, founded upon the known facts and theories of heredity, leaves the old views of fixed and absolute biological differences among the races of man, and the hierarchy of superior and inferior races founded upon this old view, without scientific justification. Biologists now agree that all men everywhere belong to a single species, *homo sapiens*..."

(Columbia Press, New York 1969, p. 163.)

These facts notwithstanding, the idea of racial superiority still grips the minds of large masses of people. It still represents one of the three greatest ideological errors of the twentieth century. These views influence the thinking not only of the people who are considered to be superior, but, oft-times, the victims. Take the case of the Black race. Although they are divided into various backgrounds and many different cultures, nonetheless there is a trend among many Black people the world over that the theory of white supremacy is ingrained in white people. That is, white people are born with this poison and nothing can ever be done to eradicate it.

The main basis for these views among Black people have been the prevalence of the theory of white superiority and the terrible treatment of people of color. The result of this unscientific approach among both Blacks and whites is that it keeps the oppressed separated from one another and helps those forces which profit from divisions among them.

As a Black American I once embraced the doctrines described above but for the last forty years I have worked closely with peoples of all colors. I had lost somewhat my sensitivity as to how deeply the roots of Black nationalism and Black separatism had penetrated among my people.

Several years ago I went to Harvard University to deliver a lecture. In the course of my stay there I visited the editor of one of the leading Black newspapers and had a long discussion. I expounded at length my views of how socialism is the answer to the problems of our oppressed people. When I finished, the editor responded by saying that on paper it would seem that what I was saying about socialism was true, but I had not answered the problem that bothered him.

"What guarantees can you give me, Mr. Lightfoot, that the white man will not betray the Black man under socialism as he has done so often under capitalism?" And then he gave the example of what had taken place in the U.S. during the Reconstruction Period after the American Civil War.

During that period, the northern capitalists made an alliance with the Black ex-slaves and together they ruled the southland for several years. But when the bourgeoisie had achieved its own goal, namely, to force the ex-slaveholders into line, it deserted the Black people and made another alliance with the slaveholders, leaving the Blacks at the tender mercies of their former masters.

The editor wanted to know if the white working class, the main social force making for socialism, found it expedient to unite today with Blacks to achieve that goal, what guarantees were there that it would not act tomorrow as did the northern bourgeoisie after the Civil War.

That thought left me almost speechless. I answered him in theoretical terms, but later it became clear to me that such answers would not suffice to meet the problems posed by racist ideology. I concluded that, among other things, it would be necessary for me to extract examples from the world as it exists today, to prove that racism is not inherent in man, that environmental, not biological factors, determine human attitudes.

And so, with the idea of uncovering all the examples I could, I made several trips to Europe, Asia, Latin America, examining situations particularly where Socialism has been established. I endeavored to show that the experiences of peoples of color in a new social setting—Socialism—would not be the same as those under capitalism.

It was with this in mind that I went to the Soviet Union in 1965 and examined in great detail how the problem had been solved in a country which under the Czar, had persecuted over two hundred different nationalities.

Then I went to Cuba, and here, again, I studied the status of Black Cubans prior to Fidel Castro, and since the Revolution. Both of these examples contained great lessons for the peoples of the world, and especially for the oppressed and persecuted, in terms of what socialism has to offer in the solution of the problems of racism.

Keeping the above firmly in mind, I wrote a book

entitled *Ghetto Rebellion to Black Liberation*, in which I pointed out how a socialist world would eliminate racism. At that time it had not yet occurred to me that perhaps one of the greatest examples that racism is not inborn, that man is influenced by environmental factors, was the existence of the two German states, one socialist and the other still under capitalism. The contrast in these two states as regards the problem of racism had not struck me forcibly until I had made two trips to Germany.

In the summer of 1970, I made a tour through both German states and I was more than ever struck by the necessity of preventing the world from ever having to live again under a rule such as Hitler's. My conviction was reinforced by observing how one people overcame racism, while the other, the West Germans, still had it in their midst although both peoples were formerly ideologically geared in the same direction.

Perhaps the incident that set off the spark was a discussion I had with a young Jewish woman by the name of Fanny who on one occasion acted as my guide. During the course of a conversation she told me the story of her life, how she had survived while 6 million of her people went to their deaths in concentration camps. She came from a wealthy Jewish family who saw the threatening clouds of fascism on the horizon and sent her to England to be out of the way of the impending catastrophe. She returned to Germany after the war only to find that her mother, father, brothers and sisters, all her relatives and friends had been destroyed by Hitler in the concentration camps. My heart went out to this woman as I listened to her story, a story that could be told by millions of other people.

But then, I was struck by something she said: "Claude, when I came back I became a teacher; now my job was to teach people who had formerly been Nazis. At first it was hard but I buckled down and did the job." My reaction was—how objective can you get? This woman, whose parents had been brutally murdered, now turned to the people who murdered them and is now teaching them, trying to show them the errors of their ways. And then it occurred to me that she could not have taught them unless she had confidence that racism was not an inborn product but an environmental force which could be changed under proper conditions.

As a result of these thoughts arising from this experience, I decided to bring to the attention of the world as much as I possibly could of what it took to produce a nation such as we now witness in the eastern part of Germany and, in so doing, to make better known experiences that will be helpful in eventually bringing about the brotherhood of all the oppressed.

But as I have said, I came away from the trip with mixed feelings. On the one hand, I was highly elated to find that after twelve years of the worst racist indoctrination any people had ever received, the people of the German Democratic Republic had largely eradicated the disease of racism from its midst. I was also happy to note that in West Germany, despite the racist program pursued by the Bonn Government, despite the outbreak of new waves of anti-Semitism, despite the drive to arm West Germany with nuclear weapons, a large section of the people are opposed to these developments. These are my most positive experiences.

On the other hand, one day as I stood near the historic boulevard, Unter den Linden, and gazed upon the spot where Hitler poisoned himself, cold chills ran down my spine as it occurred to me what an awful price mankind had to pay to put that monster in his grave. Historians estimate from 50 to 55 million dead, not to speak of the destruction of resources both natural and human. Then I recalled that despite Hitler's coming to power in Germany, it had been possible to defeat him. And I asked myself, "If an American Hitler took power in the U.S.A., would the democratic, freedom-loving forces be able to overthrow him as the allied powers had overthrown Hitler?

On his way to his grave, Hitler was prepared to carry the whole German nation down to destruction.

An American Hitler, on his way to his grave, would not hesitate to use nuclear power and attempt to destroy the entire human race.

I came away from that trip with a deeper understanding that one of the central problems before today's world is to prevent fascist-minded forces from taking complete power in the United States.

The problem becomes graver each day. Throughout the cold war years, we in the U.S. had to confront a continuous wave of fascist-like attacks upon popular liberties. Each time the resistance of the people blunted them. But, like a cancerous growth, they continue to reappear in different forms and with different methods under new personalities.

American atrocities in Vietnam, reminiscent of the Hitler era, the action of President Nixon on the Calley case, the brutal murders and frame-ups of Black and white youth, symbolized by the Angela Davis case, the murder of George Jackson and the prisoners at Attica are symptoms of a broader problem of which the question can be posed: "Whither America?" These examples and many others bring to mind again the Sinclair Lewis novel of the 1930's, *It Can't Happen Here!* In fact it is happening here. The lessons of Germany show that facism comes to power through a series of developments. It is a process.

This process is in evidence today in the United States. During several periods of post-World War II developments the danger of fascism has been manifested, but each time the threat was beaten back by popular forces. Nonetheless, the danger today is greater than ever.

There are external and internal reasons for the latest developments.

On a world scale U.S. imperialism has suffered tremendous defeats.

Almost all of its cold war objectives are in shambles. U.S. policy has been and is world domination and to save capitalism and imperialism from an aroused world.

It has pursued its goal under the "lofty" banner of preserving democracy and halting the advance of Socialism, of world Communism. Now twenty-six years after the Truman and Churchill declaration of the cold war at Fulton, Missouri, U.S.A., not only has Socialism not been rolled back, but has penetrated deeply every continent of the earth. Several years ago it was established in Cuba 90 miles from the U.S. shores. Today the Cuban example has inspired movements in the same direction throughout Latin and South America, the latest example in Chile.

The democratic pretensions of the U.S. imperialists have been unmasked as the people contrast words with deeds. Especially the lack of democracy inside the United States as it relates to Black people has been observed as a basic contradiction. The support rendered dictatorial regimes all over the world has likewise served as a measuring rod as to what U.S. imperialism has in mind for the whole world.

Another U.S. objective was to roll back and defeat the national liberation movements. This policy too, in the main, has failed. Today most of the former colonies of the major powers have won political independence and are embarking upon programs to secure economic independence.

In the pursuit of imperialist ambitions the United States has fought two wars against former colonial peoples in Korea and in Indochina. These wars have proven its power to be limited.

In both instances a most powerful military force (technically speaking) has suffered defeat at the hands of these oppressed people. In the course of these wars the American image became discredited. Today the whole world condemns what is happening in Vietnam. The reversals in the underdeveloped countries are spilling over to the European continent. The trends in Europe are away from heightening international tensions and for policies of peaceful coexistence. This fact is evidenced by the agreement between France and the Soviet Union, by the conclusion of pacts between the Federal Republic of Germany and the Soviet Union and also Poland, by the agreements around West Berlin and the general sentiment for a European security conference.

These are some of the developments of an external nature. In regards to the home front U.S. warmongers have also suffered setbacks.

During the early years of the cold war the American people in the main supported the foreign policy of the government. Most people became victims of the demagogy used by government officials. But as the years rolled by experience taught them they were greatly deceived. The disclosures of the Pentagon papers which revealed unprecedented hypocrisy have left the warmongers morally speaking completely bankrupt.

The foreign policy throughout the post-World War II years has been tied to a war economy. In the earlier stages of the cold war the economy showed to some extent an unprecedented prosperity. Today the economy is in a terrible shape and threatens drastically to reduce the standard of living of the workers and people.

Indeed a major crisis is developing in the U.S. The immoral war conducted in Vietnam, the movements of Black America for freedom, the rise of a powerful peace movement, the decline in the economy are the main factors of an internal nature. Both the external and the internal developments combine to create a political crisis. They are the background of the frenzied efforts of the Nixon administration to centralize all power into the executive branch of the government and to rule with an iron fist. They explain the desperate and brutal kind of warfare waged in Vietnam and the Black ghettos of America. They are the first steps on a path heading in the direction of a fascist police state.

In view of these developments, I came from Germany somewhat fearful about what is taking place. However, my fears calmed as I thought of the forces that could now defeat a fascist threat—that did not exist in Hitler's time.

The world is not the same as in Hitler's time. During that period the Socialist sector of the world consisted only of the Soviet people. Today over a billion people, one third of all mankind embrace Socialism and millions more are in transition from capitalism. Today political independence has been won in the former colonial world embracing over a billion and a half people. Today in the whole capitalist world there are gigantic movements for peace.

Other revolutionary forces decide the balance of world power. They are a major deterrent to U.S. imperialism. Hitler did not have to confront such an array of power until the final days of World War II. However notwithstanding these positive advantages the danger of fascism in the United States presents the world with a serious problem that must not be underestimated. Racism and anti-Communism as in the days of Adolph Hitler can still propel the world toward disaster. Hence the necessity for the people of the Western world, and the United States in particular, to grasp fully the lessons of the Third Reich.

PART I

The Background
of Fascism in Germany

CHAPTER 1

Racism and Capitalism

The time of Hitler has been described by many writers as a period in which there was a departure from Western culture and civilization. Peter Phillips, for example, wrote *The Tragedy of Nazi Germany* which is one of the best presentations of the German experience. Yet, this brilliant author cannot escape the veneer of self-righteousness which is so characteristic of most western opinion-makers. After making an impassioned plea to his countrymen to draw the lessons from Nazi Germany as insurance against a repetition of what took place in the Third Reich, he writes:

> "The monstrous enormity of Nazi crimes stuns the mind, especially one swathed in English-speaking stability and moderation."
> (Peter Phillips, *The Tragedy of Nazi Germany*, Frederick A. Praeger, Inc., New York, 1969, p. 8.)

How ridiculous! In her dealings with peoples of color over many centuries, England was anything but moderate. But then, Phillips compounds the felony when he also states:

> "But where earlier despotisms and atrocities did little more than leave a nasty taste in the mouth, Nazi tyranny and crimes against humanity shocked profoundly because they seemed to most peo-

23

ple unnatural in the twentieth century, at least in the western world."

(Ibid. p. 4.)

This example shows that even for some of those in Western countries who may be considered advanced and progressive, it is difficult to escape the virus of racist ideology. For even the attempt to play it in a low key or to evade its existence in western heritage, wittingly or unwittingly makes one an accomplice to the crime.

There have been those who have said that Hitler was representative of every German who ever lived. This was not true. For Germans, like all other peoples, have given birth to men and women who advanced the cause of humanity, as well as to those who struggled against progress. Germany gave to the world some of its best musicians, poets, philosophers, scientists—men and women who devoted their lives to the betterment of mankind. Germany gave to the world two of its finest minds—Karl Marx and Friedrich Engels. These two were men who represent all that is best in peoples of all colors and races. That is why over a billion people, a third of all in the world, live in societies which these men, more than others, defined as prerequisites to the elimination of the exploitation of man by man, nation by nation and race by race.

Surely, Hitler did not represent these. No, Hitler was not representative of every German; he was representative of all that was rotten in the social system of capitalism.

An examination of history and how it unfolded in past centuries affords evidence that the genesis of racist ideology and the racial violence that characterized the Third Reich is bound up with the development of capitalism. Many people seek to obscure this. They realize that to face up to it would call for the elimination of a society they hold dear.

This is the background which explains why so many writers who have done much to explain the phenomenon of Hitler lean over backwards to obscure the role of racism in the Third Reich and its underlying causes.

An impartial examination of history will show that before capitalism came on the scene, racist ideology did not exist. In summary, we shall, therefore, examine some other epochs in history.

Firstly, in ancient civilizations mankind had not yet evolved to the point where living things, either animal or human, had been classified as we are accustomed to do. Scientific classification of living things only started with Linnaeus in the mid-eighteenth century, and the classification of mankind on social lives a little later. J. F. Blumenbach, a pioneer anthropologist, distinguished five races in 1775: Caucasian or white, Mongolian or yellow, Ethiopian or black, American or red and Malayan or brown. These were later subdivided into categories which did not use color as the main symbol.

This does not mean that previously various peoples did not regard themselves as superior to others: they did. But whenever and wherever this attitude existed, it was not tied up with inborn racial characteristics.

Professor Kenneth Little, a participant in studies

on race conducted by UNESCO, observed the non-existence of racism in pre-capitalist society:

> "If we extend our review of culture and history beyond the area of Western civilization ... we are confronted by a very significant fact ... The virtual absence of racial relations as we define the term before the period of European overseas expansion and exploration.
> "In no other civilization ... ancient or modern do we find the kind of legal and customary recognition of group differences which characterizes the contacts of European people with other races."
> (*Race and Science*, UNESCO, New York, 1969, pp. 61–62.)

The Mexican historian, Juan Comas, gives further information on this point when he writes:

> "It may be asserted that generally speaking there was no true racial prejudice before the fifteenth century ... Before then the division of mankind was not so much into antagonistic races as into Christians and infidels, a much more humane differentiation, since the chasms between religions can be bridged while the biological racial barrier is impassable. With the beginning of African colonization and the discovery of America ... there was a considerable increase in race and color prejudice. It can be explained on grounds of economic self-interest."
> (Ibid. p. 15.)

26

These and many other authors make the point that it was capitalism which generated racism, but they do so in such vague terms that one could get the impression that the lowly exploited white masses were likewise the authors of racist ideology. Nonetheless, they have made a contribution by valuable research into these matters.

In ancient times there were those who argued that some people were born to be servants of others. Aristotle expressed this viewpoint, but he did not base this division on racial grounds.

In civilizations such as those of Egypt and Greece, the relationship between peoples of different types was that of captor and captive, of master and slave. There is little evidence of aversion or special proscription based on race or color. The Egyptians, for example, spoke scornfully of the blacks to their south, and artists sometimes caricatured black people's thick lips and woolly hair. But the Egyptians looked upon other foreigners, including blue-eyed Libyans, with equal disdain. Like earlier peoples, they mixed freely with their captives of whatever color, and some Pharaohs had mainly black features. The Greeks also had slaves, but most of them were of the same type as their masters. The Greeks did not associate any physical type with slave status. The distinction they made between peoples was cultural, not racial. They looked down on all barbarians, but if these took on Hellenistic characteristics, they were not subjected to social ostracism.

This situation was also true of the Roman Empire. Several Roman historians have described the nature of their subjected people, among them Caesar, Strabo and Tacitus. Tacitus, in particular, wrote in great detail of the character of the peoples who were put under the heel of Caesar and his legions. But these and other chroniclers of their period did not draw distinctions between subjected peoples, slaves and Romans, except on a cultural basis. No biological concepts or physical or color characteristics were advanced to indicate differences between people based on differing innate capabilities. In fact, Tacitus was impressed with the Germanic tribes.

He was a disaffected Roman moralist who was disgusted by the degeneration of Rome. He was especially impressed by the Teutonic peoples' leadership principles, and he wrote:

> "Their generals control them by example rather than by authority. If they are daring and adventurous ... they procure obedience from the admiration they inspire."
>
> (From James W. Vanderzanden, *American Minority Relations*, Ronald Press, 1963, New York, p. 128.)

The famous Roman historian, Pliny, was far from espousing racist ideas. He was very impressed by the people of Ceylon, members of the brown race who lived on a far lower cultural level. He writes:

> "They dwell in exile beyond the civilized world ... and hence are mainly free from Roman vices. They have gold and precious stones but do not use them to excess. They have

no slaves, and do not waste working hours by sleeping during daylight. The cost of living is stable, they have no civil law suits, and though it seems that crimes are not unknown, they have a splendid system of criminal jurisdiction. Their lands are well cultivated, they hunt tigers, and live for a hundred years."

(From A. N. Sherwin, *White Racial Prejudice in Imperial Rome,* Cambridge University Press, 1967, p. 39.)

Even when the Germanic tribes conquered the Roman Empire, the conquest did not result in racialist views.

Strayer describes the situation thus:

"There was a considerable amount of pillaging and violence while the Germans were moving through the empire, but once they had settled down they were not hostile to the Romans. There had never been any deep rooted racial or cultural antagonism between Romans and Germans."

(Joseph R. Strayer, *Western Europe in the Middle Ages,* Appleton Century Crofts, New York, 1955, p. 29.)

They were not very different in the time of the feudal regimes. In the early days of the traffic in slaves off the West Coast of Africa, the racist virus had not yet taken hold. The Portuguese, who were the first to travel along the African coast and engage in trade, including slaves, did not view the problem as one of dealing with an inferior people.

29

Moore writes:

> "When the Portuguese and others first made contact with the native states of West Africa, they found a culture there which they felt they could understand and appreciate. The feudal nature of the West African kingdoms was enough like that of fifteenth century Europe for the Europeans to recognize the system and to feel at home in it . . ."

(Clark D. Moore, *A Survey of the Past*, Bantam Pathfinder, New York, 1968, p. 117.)

He also shows why this attitude was replaced by another:

> "A radical change in the relationship came about with the development of the large-scale slave trade. This worked in several ways to change the European attitude toward Africans. The European had to justify the trade to himself by assuming the inferiority of the African, thus persuading himself that it was part of God's plan that 'lesser breeds' work for the superior races. This became increasingly easy as more and more Europeans came into contact with Africans —Africans who had become thoroughly debased and dehumanized by enslavement. Thus, the continent's population came to be judged by Europeans in terms of the uprooted and shattered fragments of humanity which were the stock in trade of the slaving business."

(Ibid. p. 118.)

The character of slavery, as it now developed under capitalism and gave rise to racism, is summed up by J. L. Hammond and B. Hammond. They write:

"... The West Indian slave trade was in this sense worse than the slave trade of the ancient world, for the slave brought from Delos to Italy was originally, in theory, an enemy whose life had been spared; but the slave carried to Jamaica was so much muscle to be appropriated and used by anybody strong enough to seize it. He was not a human being who had lost his rights in battle, but a piece of merchandise; he had no more in the way of human rights than a bar of iron, or a mass of lumber picked up by a wanderer on the sea shore."

(I. L. and B. Hammond, *The Rise of Modern Industry*, Harcourt, Brace and World, Inc., 1926, New York, p. 62.)

The reasons for the birth of racism which coincided with the rise of capitalism, have been pointed out by a large number of influential students of history, both Black and white, such as Sir Eric Williams and Ashley Montagu.

The historian Montagu gave further evidence of the source of racism:

"A study of the documents of the English and American slave traders down to the eighteenth century also serves to show that these men held no other conception of their victims than that, by virtue of their position as slaves, they were socially their inferior. But that was not all, *for many of these hard-hearted, hard-bitten men* recorded their belief that their victims were often quite clearly their mental equals and superior to many in their own homes.

"It was only when voices began to make themselves heard against the inhuman traffic in slaves . . . that, on the defensive, the supporters of slavery were forced to look about them for opponents . . . The champions of slavery could only attempt to show that the slaves were most certainly not as good as their masters. And in this highly charged emotional atmosphere there began doleful recitation of the catalog of differences which were alleged to prove the inferiority of the slave to his master."

(Ashley Montagu, *Man's Most Dangerous Myth, the Fallacy of Race,* Columbia University Press, New York, 1945, pp. 34–35.)

Among the distinguished scholars who have discovered capitalism as the source of racism are a number of scientists who participated in the international forums conducted by UNESCO. Invaluable contributions were made by the Mexican historian Juan Comas, who wrote a booklet on *Racial Myths*, Kermitt Little in *Race and Society*, Michel Leiris in *Race and Culture*, L. C. Dunn in *Race and Biology*, and a host of others. In these well-documented works it is shown to be a scientifically proven fact that there are no inferior or superior races.

At its birth, capitalism committed some of the most

barbaric acts and genocidal treatment of people ever seen. It is estimated by historians that 60 to 80 million people died in Africa to bring 20 million slaves to the New World. It is well documented that genocidal treatment of the American Indian was as bad as anything any human beings ever did to others.

If anyone has any illusions that genocide began in the Third Reich, he may read what Sloan uncovered from the memoirs of a soldier:

"About daybreak on the morning of the 29th of November we came in sight of the camp of the friendly Indians aforementioned, and were ordered by Colonel Chivington to attack the same, which was accordingly done ... the village of the Indians consisted of from one hundred to one hundred and thirty lodges, and, as far as I am able to judge, of from five hundred to six hundred souls, the majority of which were women and children; in going over the battle-ground the next day I did not see a body of man, woman or child but was scalped, and in many instances their bodies were mutilated in the most horrible manner--men, women, and children's private parts cut out, etc.: I heard one man say that he had cut out a woman's private parts and had them for exhibition on a stick ... according to the best of my knowledge and belief these atrocities that were committed were with the knowledge of J. M. Chivington, and I do not know of his taking any measures to prevent them; I heard of one instance of a child a few months old being thrown in the feedbox of a wagon and after being carried some distance, left on the ground to perish; I also heard of numerous instances in which men had cut the private parts of females and stretched them over the saddle-bows, and wore them over their hats while riding in the ranks . . ."

(Irving J. Sloan, *Our Violent Past,* Random House, New York, 1970, pp. 20–21.)

Sloan devotes his entire book to cataloging incidents such as that described above. The following is another example:

"When it was day the soldiers returned to the fort—considering that they had done a deed of Roman valour, in murdering so many in their sleep, where infants were torn from their mothers breast and hacked to pieces in the presence of their parents and the pieces thrown into the fire . . . and other sucklings then cut, stuck and pierced."

(Ibid. p. 17.)

These examples of savage brutality come from American history. As a nation our past has been as cruel, as bereft of humanity as anything which occurred in the Nazi concentration camps. And when I read about them, unlike Peter Phillips, they do more than leave "a nasty taste in the mouth."

Furthermore, if anyone has any illusions that brutalities in modern times were a peculiar German phenomenon of Hitlerism or only occurred in early

American history, let them examine the nature of the atrocities committed by American forces today in Vietnam. Dr. U Thant, former Secretary-General of the United Nations, has characterized the war waged there by U.S. imperialism as the worst in human history.

It may justly be said that U.S. imperialism does not need gas chambers; it has napalm bombs and, as a result of their usage and other horrible techniques, over half a million civilians—men, women and children—have been killed, maimed or wounded. Millions more have been uprooted from their homes and have witnessed the systematic destruction of their land, so that it will probably not be productive for many years to come.

Wholesale murder of men, women and children is an almost daily occurrence. The example given by an S.S. officer in Germany who picked up a little Jewish child, threw her into the air and then shot her to amuse his little daughter, is repeated by Lt. Calley who threw a Vietnamese child into a ditch and shot the child to death.

The situation has become so bad that even Telford Taylor, chief prosecutor at the Nuremberg trials, was compelled to condemn the atrocities by U.S. forces. He declared:

"As one who until 1965 supported American intervention in Vietnam ... I am painfully aware of the instability of individual judgement ... How could it ever be thought that air strikes, free-fire zones and a mass uprooting and

removal of the rural population were the way to win the allegiance of the South Vietnamese."
(Telford Taylor, *Nuremberg and Vietnam, an American Tragedy*, Bantam, New York, 1971, p. 206.)

He further stated the Vietnam war to be

". . . the most costly and tragic national blunder in American history. And so it has come to this: that the anti-aggression spirit of Nuremberg and the U.N. Charter is invoked to justify our venture in Vietnam, where we have smashed the country to bits, and will not even take the trouble to clean up the blood and rubble. None will ever thank us . . . somehow we failed ourselves to learn the lessons we undertook to teach at Nuremberg and that failure is today's American tragedy."
(Ibid. p. 207.)

Such is the history of racism and racial violence in so-called Western civilization. Hitler understood his own relationship to it when he wrote:

"The so-called white race has created for itself a privileged position in the world. I am quite unable to understand . . . this economic supremacy of the white race over the rest of the world if I do not bring into close connection a political conception of supremacy which has been peculiar to the white race for many centuries and has been regarded as in the nature of things. This conception it has maintained in its dealings with other peoples. Take any area you like. Take, for example, India. England did not conquer India by the way of justice and law; she conquered India without regard to the wishes, the views of the natives or to their formulations of justice, and when necessary she has upheld this supremacy with the most brutal ruthlessness ... Just in the same way Cortez or Pizarro annexed Central America ... Not on any basis of any claim of right, but from the absolute inborn feeling of the superiority of the white race ... It matters not what superficial disguises in individual cases this right may have assumed in practice of an extraordinarily brutal right to dominate others, and from this political conception was developed the basis for the economic annexation of that world which was not inhabited by the white race."

(*Speeches of Adolf Hitler*, 1922–1939, U. W. Bayne, Howard Fertig, New York 1969, p. 792.)

The foregoing should suffice to show that charges that Hitler departed from Western traditions are false and without foundation. Hitler learned his racist concepts from Western capitalism and accelerated them.

The problem of environmental or hereditary factors is basic. Today, twenty-seven years after the defeat of the Nazis, there appears another interpretation of the hereditary factors in the United States.

The new theories are not openly racist. They are a

37

direct response to the gigantic peace movement that is sweeping the U.S. and the world today. They are attempting to derail it. The same propositions which are advanced to suggest that man is inherently violent provide a rationale for continued racial violence.

During the last ten years, there appeared on the American scene a number of books, such as *The African Genesis* by Robert Ardrey in 1961, and five years later, *The Territorial Imperative*. A third book, *The Social Contract*, has just been published. In addition to Ardrey, there are other authors who endeavor to show man's animal heritage as the main backdrop for his killing instincts. Among these are, *On Aggression* by Konrad Lorenz, and *The Naked Ape* by Desmond Morris. These authors come from different backgrounds but they agree that wars do not emanate from economic and social causes but from biological aggressiveness. The chief among these writers is Robert Ardrey, whose controversial book, *The African Genesis*, is widely circulated. His thesis is that man's supposed disposition to violence and the subjugation of others was inherited from his animal background millions of years ago. He wrote:

> "Any animal with a capacity for learning must in part be a product of his environment. Any animal with a capacity for hunger must in part be dominated by economic motives. But to believe that the fascination with war and weapons, or the imagined accomplishment of a perfect crime, or unyielding temptation to lord it over somebody or everlasting drives to acquire

UNIVERSITY OF WINNIPEG
LIBRARY
515 Portage Avenue
DISCARDED

someone else's wealth—to believe that such as
these find their source in human society and may
be exorcized forever with environmental manipulation, is to make of a man a most modest black-
board on which any other may write his name."
(Robert Ardrey, *The African Genesis*, Dell Publishing Co., New York, 1961, p. 159.)

If this view is accepted, then there is no point in
building a peace movement; there is no point in
seeking to overcome racism, because its basic roots
are to be found in the biological nature of man, inherited since time immemorial.

The appearance of these books and their wide
circulation require further discussion. It is clear that
the elimination of racism will not be simple. Racism,
as we have already stated, was born out of economic
necessity for the capitalist class. It was profitable for
those who promoted it. Nonetheless, in time, it became one of the institutions of capitalism. Thus, it
will not be easy to eradicate. To eliminate it completely will require persistent efforts over a long time,
above all proper education.

The rationale behind the present wave of exponents
of the hereditary aspect was provided many years ago
by the American philosopher, John Dewey, who, in
"Does Human Nature Change?", wrote:

"The assertion that human nature cannot be
changed is heard when social changes are urged
as reforms and improvements of existing conditions. It is always heard when the proposed

39

changes in institutions or conditions stand in sharp opposition to what exists . . ."
(*Rotarian*, February 1938.)

In reference to the combative instincts of man, which Ardrey says come from his animal heritage, John Dewey observed:

"I have always said that, in my opinion, combativeness is a constituent part of human nature. But I have also said that the manifestations of these native elements are subject to change because they are affected by custom and tradition. War does not exist because man has combative instincts, but because social conditions and forces have led, almost forced, these 'instincts' into this channel."
(Ibid.)

The differences between man and animal were also elaborated on with great skill by L. C. Dunn:

"In man, ability to succeed in a great variety of environments is connected with the most important way in which he differs from lower animals, that is, his ability to learn and to profit by experience and especially to live in organized societies and to develop culture. The religious, moral and ethical traditions which all societies develop in some form, language which permits oral and written communication between generations and between different societies, the evolution of political and economic institutions and of literature, art, science, technology and industry—all of these reflect the peculiar mental adaptability and plasticity of man. All civilizations increase the selective advantage of genes for mental capacity and educability and these are found in all races."

(L. C. Dunn, *Race and Science*, Columbia Press, 1969, p. 293.)

CHAPTER 2

Germany, Fascism and Racism before 1945

After the foundation of the Second German Reich with the strong military power Prussia as backbone in 1871, capitalist industry developed at an unprecedented rate, and by the turn of the century Germany had become one of the most powerful industrial nations in the world. By 1910, she was Europe's leading iron and steel producer, although less than forty years earlier her output had been far below that of Great Britain. In 1847, Germany had a small mercantile fleet estimated at 8,944 gross tons; by 1913, she had 2,098 ships with a tonnage of 4,380,000; between 1872 and 1913, her exports more than quadrupled and imports almost tripled. In new industries such as chemicals, electrical goods and automobiles, Germany became a world leader. In a period of a little more than one generation, she was transformed from an agrarian society to a modern, highly efficient industrialized and urbanized nation, and in this respect became a serious challenge to England in her long-time position as the "workshop of the world."

Germany's industrialization was marked by a concentration of large-scale units of finance, production and distribution. Powerful finance and individual corporations dominated the scene, whose rulers, in close alliance with the landowning and officer class of Prussia, increasingly strove to turn Germany into a first-rate world empire, with colonial possessions, markets, spheres of influence etc. second to none.

As a result, Germany now took the path of imperialist expansion of re-dividing the world. This process arose out of the very logic of capitalism, a law of capitalism. Imperialism is a stage of capitalism that comes on the scene of history when monopolies, ruling supreme, have replaced free competition, and when colonial expansion is no longer possible without wars between the great powers, since the globe has been carved up.

At the close of the century, Germany had reached the point where either she had to expand or die as a growing capitalist power.

Lenin described the situation as follows:

"On the other hand, opposed to this group, mainly Anglo-French, stands another group of capitalists, even more predatory and more piratical—a group which came to the capitalist feasting board when all the places had been taken, but which introduced into the struggle new methods of developing capitalist production, better technique, incomparable organization, which transformed the old capitalism, the capitalism of the epoch of free competition, into the capitalism of gigantic trusts, syndicates and cartels. This group introduced the principle of state capitalist production, uniting the gigantic forces of capitalism with the gigantic forces of the states into one mechanism, and amalgamating tens of millions of

43

people in a single organization of state capitalism."

(V. I. Lenin, *War and the Workers*, International
Publishers, New York, 1940, p. 10.)

Lenin summed up the events leading to the outbreak
of World War I, and later to the Third Reich, when
he wrote:

". . . A new robber appeared. In 1871 a new capitalist power arose, which developed ever so
much faster than England. This is a fundamental
fact. You will not find a single book on economic
history that does not admit this indisputable fact
–Germany's more rapid development. This rapid
development of German capitalism was the development of a young and strong robber, who
came before the League of European Powers and
said: 'You ruined Holland, you defeated France,
you have taken half the world–please give us our
share.'"

(Ibid. p. 11.)

The combination of these trends in German history,
coupled with the events that erupted with great inten-
sity between the two world wars, are the main elements to which the whole picture of what transpired
in the Third Reich must be related. The failure to do
this can lead only to erroneous conclusions about all
other related phenomena present. Racist ideology and
violence as unfolded in Germany were a by-product
of these developments, but inasmuch as racism was
one of the main ideological weapons utilized by Hit-

ler, it must be considered a central aspect of the lessons to be drawn from the German experience.

To work for a program to combat racist ideology, one must look into its economic and political background. One must know who benefits from it and why. This is fundamental to an understanding of the conditions required to overcome it.

In this respect, the post-World War II developments in the two German states—the German Democratic Republic of Eastern Germany and the Federal Republic of Western Germany—provide a laboratory of experience.

The post-World War I years were characterized by revolutionary upheavals in many countries. They began with the Russian Revolution of 1917, which marked the beginning of the end of the system of capitalism. It was followed by the revolution in Germany of 1918. At the war's end, the soldiers left the battle front and, together with the workers, overthrew the Kaiser and his government. This revolution stopped short of worker's power—there was no transition to socialism but only the establishment of a weak bourgeois democracy. Had there been a successful socialist revolution, mankind would have been spared the holocaust of Hitler's fascism.

But the crisis was not confined to these two countries. All over the world the working class went into struggle, and this revolutionary situation did not subside until about 1923.

Afterward there was apparent stabilization in most countries, including Germany. But to achieve this partial stabilization, some concessions were granted to the working class. This was in the form of unemployment insurance, medical aid and other welfare provisions.

However, the period of stabilization did not last long. In 1929, a world economic crisis broke out. Capitalism periodically had given birth to crises of overproduction, but none had been nearly as bad as this one, which deeply affected all capitalist countries and Germany more than any other.

The German economic crisis not only affected the workers but also brought about the downfall of the middle class, already impoverished by the war and the inflation. Keynes, a liberal capitalist economist, stated on the latter:

> ". . . pre-war savings of the middle class, so far as they were invested in bonds, mortgages or bank deposits, have been largely or entirely wiped out."
> (R. Palme Dutt, *Fascism and Social Revolution*, International Publishers, New York, 1935, p. 105.)

The effects of the crisis on professionals were unprecedented. The Prussian Minister of Education reports that out of 22,000 teachers who completed their training, only 990 found jobs. According to H. H. Tiltman in *Slump*, "Engineers have become mere wage-earners while of the technical school engineering graduates only one in five found any job at all."

The crisis was even sharper among workers, and by 1932 8 million were unemployed in a nation of 60 million. Between 1929 and 1932, official figures show total wages and salaries fell from 44.5 billion to 25.7 billion marks. Unemployment benefits were cut heavily. Most concessions granted during partial stabilization were wiped out and, in addition, taxes on low-income groups greatly increased.

Germany, like other capitalist countries, showed that the ruling capitalists had determined to put the burden of the crisis on the masses. While living standards of low income groups declined, profits for the ruling class were normal and in some instances increased. In other cases, where the ruling class was affected adversely, the government apparatus helped bail these sectors out. This was universal. In the first years in the U.S., Hoover primed the pump giving corporations many exemptions and much financial aid. In Germany big landowners and Junkers (owners of agricultural estates in the Eastern provinces) were deeply affected by the crisis. The government came to their aid with a slush fund and by 1932 they had received 4 billion marks.

The economic situation became so grave in Germany that it led to a political crisis and within that context provided a chance for Hitler to take power. Dutt writes:

"What led to this sudden expansion of Fascism in Germany in 1930–1932? The world economic crisis, which undermined the basis of stabilization and of the Weimar Republic, undermined equally the position of Social Democracy which was closely linked up with these... Capitalism in Germany required to advance to new methods in

47

the face of the crisis. It required to wipe out the remainder of the social gains of the revolution, in respect to social legislation, hours and wages, which had constituted the main basis of influence of Social Democracy in the working class and its stock-in-trade to point to as the fruits of its policy. In place of the concessions of the early years of the revolution, capitalism required now to advance to Draconian economic measures against the workers. For this purpose new forms of intensified dictatorship were necessary."
(Ibid. p. 137.)

Until the outbreak of this crisis, the governments of the Weimar Republic had rested on coalitions of various bourgeois parties with the Social Democrats. This was possible because the Social-Democratic Party, while standing for socialism, did nothing to advance it. The Social-Democratic Party did not disturb the forces behind the government—the big industrialists, the Junkers, and military.

But with the new situation, when there was no relief in sight, the ruling circles concluded that to transfer the burden of the crisis to the masses would require strong governmental action—the ability to break the working class parties and the trade union movement.

To achieve these goals, the ruling class could no longer rely on the rule by parliament and on coalitions in which the Social Democrats played a leading part. The 1930 elections prepared the way for a new alignment of forces: They revealed the new trend of an enormous growth in influence of the National Socialist

Party of Hitler and at the same time substantial gains of the Communist Party. They also showed a decline of the Social-Democratic Party:

> "Results of the Reichstag elections of September 14, 1930: Social-Democrats 8,572,000 votes; Nazis 6,401,000; Communists 4,590,000; Centrists 4,129,000; German Nationalists 2,458,000; German People's Party 1,658,000; Agrarian and Conservative (a split-off of the Nationalists) 1,563,000; Economy Party 1,379,000; State Party (former Democrats) 1,323,000; Bavarian People's Party 1,058,000."
> (Ibid.)

The growth of the Hitler Party indicates the beginning of a regrouping of class forces leading to a fascist dictatorship. The first decisive steps on this road were taken by the Brüning Government, in office since early 1930. Brüning, who lacked a majority in parliament, held office by virtue of "the confidence of the President," the Kaiser's aged Field Marshal von Hindenburg, and governed by emergency decrees without parliamentary assent.

The Social-Democratic Party, the strongest in parliament, acceded to this, thus contributing to the first major step making it possible for Hitler, upon assuming the presidency, to finish wiping out all democratic processes.

The trend noted in the 1930 election results continued in the years to follow. The economic situation deteriorated further and sharpened the political spectrum considerably. The Nazi and Communist Parties both continued to gain strength. This is also indicated in the election returns of 1932 and 1933. They revealed that the Communist Party still continued to gain support and that the Social-Democratic Party declined.

These developments were the immediate and direct cause of the ruling circles' decision to bring Hitler to power. Events moved rapidly in such a way that, given a few more years of similar developments, there would have been a fair chance that Germany would have taken the path of the Russian Revolution of 1917 and would have ushered in a socialist reorganization of society. The ruling class had to choose between a transition to socialism and maintaining capitalism by a fascist dictatorship.

Thus, the clash between the two social systems—capitalism and socialism—was the root cause of Hitler's coming to power in 1933. At that moment in history, Germany represented the weakest link in the chain of world imperialism and the bourgeoisie felt compelled to act.

The dismantling of democracy could have been prevented if unity had been created between the Communist and Social-Democratic Parties. In the first election campaign of 1932, their combined vote was about 14 million. Had there been such unity, it would have attracted millions of vacillating elements. It is conceivable that, instead of the Third Reich, a Socialist Germany would have been the order of the day. At least, there would have been the maintenance of a more democratic system.

In this crisis, the Social-Democratic Party acted as

it had done throughout the whole period of the Weimar Republic. It considered its alliance with the Junkers, the military and the bourgeoisie of more importance than an alliance with the Communists. Indeed, in the fateful presidential campaign of March 1932, the Social-Democratic Party withdrew its own candidate, rejected the united front appeal of the Communists and supported Hindenburg on the theory of the lesser evil, an action that later proved fatal, because Hindenburg turned power over to Hitler.

Hindenburg appointed Hitler chancellor when the fascist vote had decreased by 2 million and that of the Communists had increased. In the elections of November 1932 the German fascist party gained 11.7 million of the votes, as against 13.2 million for the two working class parties. The ruling circles were afraid that Nazi electoral successes had passed their summit.

The results of the election of late 1932, the last in which the Communists could seriously compete although Nazi terror ruled the streets in many German cities and villages, show that Hitler by no means had the support of the majority of the people. His ability to transform large sections of Germans into willing accomplices and to win over majority support resulted from events which occurred after he took power. In this, he was aided by three main factors:

First, the economic situation. When Hitler took power, there were 6 million unemployed, which included a large sector of the former middle class elements, professionals, etc. By 1937 the number was one million. Hitler placed the country on a war economy and promised to solve the economic problems especially of the middle class. The unemployed were either conscripted into the army or semi-military organisations or put into armament factories. Many had become demoralized and were ready to seek relief no matter what methods were used.

But it was not only the corrupt and declassed elements within German society who were attracted to Hitler's program. Many other people were impressed by the decrease in unemployment and took the Nazi propaganda about "German socialism" and the need to exclude the Jewish minority from German life seriously.

Another factor rallying support to Hitler was military success, initially achieved without a general war. Beginning with the remilitarization of the Rhineland, he succeeded in occupying Austria and Czecho-Slovakia (in both cases) aided by the Western powers; the quick conquest of Poland and France and the subjugation of large parts of Europe made Hitler appear the most successful German military leader of all times.

These conquests, which resulted in looting other countries and dragging their people off to slave in German factories, mills and mines, corrupted considerable parts of the German people, who were allowed a small share of the spoils and could bask in the idea that they were lording it over all other nations.

Hitler was able also to secure a mass base among German youth. The new generation of youth had not experienced the horrors of World War I. They had felt the full weight of the economic crisis, unemployment and the disintegration of the Weimar Republic. Without prospects for the future, they became receptive to Nazi demagogy and promises that Germany would have a place in the sun.

Last not least the fascist regime ruled absolute by the highly organized and rigid suppression of all democratic and socialist opposition, all working class and democratic organizations. This suppression was from the very beginning practiced with methods of terror: It began with the murder of hundreds and the imprisonment of tens of thousands of opponents and culminated in the physical extinction of almost all active anti-fascists who had not left the country. These facts are so well-known that there is no need to go further into this matter here, except to stress that persecution of all opponents served to intimidate many millions of Germans who would otherwise have refused to cooperate with the Nazis. Through a combination of such factors Hitler was able to consolidate his power and win support for his class and racist policies.

Regarding the many causes for Hitler's success, only few writers in Western countries have placed them against the background of the real meaning of fascism, what it represents and what the international situation was which made it possible for fascism to be successful in Germany. Some of the most asinine explanations have been given as to the nature of fascism. There have been those who characterized it as a revolt of the middle class—thus obscuring the role of the big monopolies. There have been those who characterized fascism merely as the instrument of the military, thus ignoring the role of the big monopolies. Even a scholar of the caliber of Golo Mann did not understand the specific nature of fascism. In typical abstract liberal fashion, he wrote:

> "What then was National Socialism? It was an historically unique phenomenon, dependent on an individual and on a moment, a phenomenon which can never reappear in the same form. It was a state of intoxication by a gang of intoxicated experts, kept up for a few years. It was a machine for the manufacture of power ... used to fuel German energies, German interests, passions and ideas ..."
>
> (Golo Mann, *The History of Germany Since 1789*, Frederick A. Praeger, New York 1968, p. 446.)

In his Marxist anylysis, Dutt correctly says:

> "Fascism is the outcome of modern capitalism in crisis, of capitalism passing into the period of proletarian revolution, when it can no longer maintain its power by the old means, but is compelled to resort to ever more violent methods for the suppression of all working class organisation, and also for the attempted authoritarian economic unification and organisation of its own anarchy, in a last desperate effort to maintain its existence and master the contradictions that are rending it."
>
> (R. Palme Dutt, *Fascism and Social Revolution*, International Publishers, New York, 1935, p. 290.)

The reader will note that Dutt defines fascism as the outcome of modern capitalism in crisis, and not just of German capitalism. It is quite true that Hitler's rise to power was also due to the leading agencies of international capitalism—especially the major Western powers. Eventually they waged war against Hitler and his regime, but this was not of their choosing. They would have preferred that Hitler play the role they had consigned to him—to attack the Soviet Union. But capitalism is capitalism, and while its major contradiction is between it and the socialist system, the various capitalist powers have contradictions amongst themselves.

The Western powers, prior to Hitler's war against France, had sought to change the situation, to make it possible for Hitler to march his hordes east and not west. This was the meaning of the appeasement policies at Munich. Regarding this, the Italian historian Gaetano Salvemini wrote:

> "The leaders of the Conservative Party and the British foreign office deceived the British people throughout 1935. The British leaders had reached an understanding with Hitler which allowed him a free hand toward Russia, thus making World War II unavoidable."
> (D. F. Fleming, *The Cold War and Its Origin*, Doubleday, New York 1961, pp. 36–37.)

With the aim of an attack on the Soviet Union, the allied powers helped to rebuild the German economy. Such objectives were behind the economic collaboration that had existed with Germany over a long period, and especially the penetration of American capital into German finance and industrial capital. The extent to which this was accomplished is seen in a letter written by Alfred P. Sloan, Chairman of General Motors, on April 6, 1939, which reads in part:

> "General Motors is an international organization. It operates in practically every country in the world . . . many years ago, General Motors—before the present regime in Germany—invested a large amount of money in Adam Opel A.G. It has been a very profitable investment, and I think outside of the political phase, its future potentiality from the standpoint of development and profit, is equal to, if not greater than many other investments the Corporation has made. It enjoys about 50 percent of the business in Germany—a little less than that to be exact. It employs German workers and consumes German materials . . .
>
> "Having attained the position which we have, through evolution, hard work, and, I believe, intelligent management, or approaching 50 percent of one of the most important industries in Germany, I feel that we must conduct ourselves as a German organization, involving German capital . . ."
>
> (Albert Kahn, *The Plot Against the Peace*, Dial Press, Inc. New York, 1945, p. 32.)

In the years 1924–28, 63 billion marks were invested in German industry. Over 30 billion came from abroad, especially from the U.S. This bolstering of the German economy was the basis for the enormous modernized war machine that Hitler built.

Thus, fascism is an international phenomenon. It occurred in Germany because that country was the weakest link in the chain of world capitalism.

Many writers have dealt with the period between the two world wars. However, most have done so without viewing the picture as a whole. Moreover, they have treated that period in isolation from the historical development of Germany which does present special features and problems. Conversely, most writers who have analyzed the historical aspect have done so out of context with the realities of the world situation between 1914 and 1933. To grasp the fundamentals of the German experience, it is essential to tie in history with the current situation. Otherwise, there can be no full understanding of why Germany took the path she did, why racism played such a large role in Hitler's propaganda, why so many Germans followed Hitler and wrought such havoc.

Since racism and racial violence are by-products of capitalism and imperialism, existing long before Hitler, certain questions arise: What did he add that was not there before? What effect did he have on the German mind? And finally, what were some of the conditions and methods he utilized to mobilize the German people behind his barbaric program?

Many authors who have written about the German experience have characterized the German people as having a natural bent for cruelty. On this basis they analyzed the causes for what took place during the Hitlerian era. This concept that the German people were a mentally unstable and cruel people must be rejected. But, while doing so, we must realize that something did happen to the minds of very many Germans during Hitler's regime. He made them believe that they were the master race.

His racial theories were in part rooted in the doctrines of Gobineau, the French historian who added a biological aspect to the concept of racial superiority and inferiority.

Gobineau consigned most of the human race to the status of inferior people. This included the black, yellow, brown and most white people. His view on the Aryan type fitted the description of many Teutonic peoples but not all. His theories first advanced during the fifties of the nineteenth century, were later used by the ideologues of imperialism primarily against people of color.

Hitler carried forward Gobineau's theories of Aryan superiority and added to racist ideology anti-Communism. Racism in previous centuries did not contain this dual character because the class question had not yet developed to that point. The Russian Revolution of 1917 ushered in a new era, providing an example of how the whole system, imperialism, colonialism and racism, could be destroyed. It showed that the struggle to establish socialism is the basic condition to end racism and racial violence. The ideologues of German fascism grasped this fundamental truth and combined racism and anti-Communism in a common ideology. Thus the propaganda campaign waged in the Third Reich pictured the class struggle as symptom of a basic racial struggle.

As a Black American, I have experienced racism since birth. Forty years of my life have been devoted to work as a Black American Communist. I know from first hand experience what it means to have racism and anti-Communism involved in persecution. The combination of these two ideological poisons brings into existence a far greater and more intensive form of racist or class persecution.

Throughout his entire career, Hitler never deviated in placing these two questions in the same category because he understood the implications. That he understood this relationship is evidenced by the following statement made to a Nuremberg conference on September 12, 1938, when he declared:

> "When the question is still put to us why national socialism fights with such fanaticism against the Jewish element in Germany, why it pressed and still presses for its removal ... because *we can never suffer an alien race ... claim the leadership of our working class.*"
> (*Hitler Speaks*, Oxford University Press, New York, 1942, p. 735.)

This is the reason why Hitler, at all times in his propaganda campaigns, never failed to link the Jews with the problems of Bolshevism or Communism. Hitler understood what unfortunately many people who suffer from racist and capitalist oppression do not understand, namely, that unity of class, national and racial struggles is the Achilles heel of capitalism and imperialism.

Hitler sought to transform Europe into a colony

of German imperialism. He also had plans for Africa, etc., but his first objective was Europe and the subjugation of all Slavs, who totaled hundreds of millions of people. An example of his plan was given in a reference to Russians, when he stated, "Treat those nigger people like slaves. Make them Germany's colonial Africa." (Viereck, *Roots of the Nazi Mind*, Capricorn Books, New York, 1965, p. 342.)

To carry forward his plans to transform Europe into a colony, Hitler first had to convince the German people that it was dealing with "wild animals." In this regard, long before he came to power, he had stated very clearly his concept of Jews and Slavs. In *Mein Kampf*, he wrote:

> "In the Jewish people, the will to sacrifice one-self does not go beyond the bare instinct of self-preservation ... The seemingly great feeling of belonging together is rooted in a very primitive herd instinct, as it shows itself in a similar way in many other living beings in this world. Thereby, the fact is remarkable that in all these cases, a common herd instinct leads to mutual support only as long as a common danger makes this seem useful or unavoidable. The same pack of wolves, that jointly falls upon its booty dissolves when its hunger abates. The same is true of horses, which try to ward off the attacker in common, and which fly in different directions when the danger is gone ...
>
> "With Jews the case is similar. His will to sacrifice is only ostensible. It endures only as long as

the existence of the individual absolutely requires this. However, as soon as the common enemy is beaten and the danger threatening all is averted, the booty recovered, the apparent harmony among the Jews themselves ceases to make way again for the inclinations originally present. The Jew remains united only if forced by a common danger or is attracted by a common booty; if both reasons are no longer evident, then the qualities of the crassest egoism come into their own and, in a moment, the united people become *a horde of rats, fighting bloodily among themselves*."

(Adolf Hitler, *Mein Kampf*, Raynal and Hitchcock, New York, 1940, pp. 414–16.)

His view of the Slavs was no different and he made many statements regarding them as no more than wild animals.

This viewpoint was propagated in thousands of books and forced on the German people. Never before was there such a concentrated racist propaganda as during the twelve years of Hitler's regime. As a consequence, a considerable part of the German people became convinced of the biological inferiority of people of "non-Aryan stock" and thus were prepared to carry out the horrible crimes that took place in the concentration camps and elsewhere. However, most Germans did not realize that they would have to pay an awful price for embracing his racist and chauvinist views.

Another weapon utilized by the fascists was fear.

Terror against Germans preceded Buchenwald, Auschwitz and the wholesale destruction of Jews and Slavs. Concentration camps were established and anti-fascists were jailed or forced into exile. Over 500,000 Germans were thrown into concentration camps. Neighbor was turned against neighbor and families were split up – children were used against parents. The world was horrified at what happened to Jews and Slavs, but it must also note that a pre-requisite was what Hitler did to Germans in the first place. After eliminating all opposition and taking complete power, he transformed every institution of mass education into a means of inculcating fascist ideas. Prior to his coming to power *Mein Kampf* was sold in few copies. Later it became the German bible. The works of some of the foremost thinkers and scholars—people who had done much to advance the culture of the entire world, including many famous German writers—were tossed into the flames in Berlin on the evening of May 10, 1933. The media of mass publicity were molded into a gigantic machinery to propagate Nazi views and to dehumanize the people.

A. L. Kenny wrote in the *New York Times*, October 1938:

> "Every German is expected to read *Mein Kampf*, and every young married couple is presented with a copy; it is a best-seller with a sale to date of 5 million copies . . .
>
> "Furthermore, all political texts took their cues from *Mein Kampf*. No teacher or lecturer would dare to state views at variance with its spirit."

On September 22, 1933, the Reich Chamber of Culture was set up under Goebbels who, together with the fascist ideologue Rosenberg, attempted to obtain complete control over the thoughts of the nation. Throughout this period of intensive propaganda a central feature was to remove all human instincts from the people and arouse only those feelings needed for wars of aggression and for pitiless treatment of other peoples. Hitler admitted his goal when he wrote:

> "My pedagogy is hard. The weak must be chiseled away ... I want a violent, arrogant, unafraid cruel youth, who must be able to suffer pain ... Thus I can create the new. I do not want an intellectual education ... They shall learn to overcome the fear of death through the most arduous tests ..."

Thus the whole education system was geared to bring this condition about. Educational standards were lowered as Hitler transformed educational institutions into training centers for dehumanization. During this period, university students dropped in number by over half, to 58,325. It is also estimated that among those enrolled in the institutes of technology, from which many of Germany's most famous scientists and engineers had come, the decline was even greater. Hitler did not care about the decline in public school because he counted more on Nazi youth organizations. The fascists built up very powerful youth organizations which finally embraced 10 million young people. The concordat of July 20, 1933, provided that all German Catholic youth join the Hitler youth movement. German youth were to be educated physically, intellectually and morally in the spirit of National Socialism. Children from 6 to 10 were required to take the following oath:

> "In the presence of this blood banner which represents our Führer I swear to devote all my energies and strength to the savior of our country, Adolf Hitler. I am willing and ready to give my life for him so help me God!"

As indicated, fear was injected into the nation to achieve Hitler's purpose and it is reported that if parents were found guilty of preventing their children from joining fascist-led youth organizations, they were subject to heavy prison sentences. Thus a far-reaching influence over the minds of youth and children was established and used to transform many young people into fanatical fascists and racists prepared to commit any crime against other peoples.

PART II

The German Democratic Republic
Shows The Way to Survival

CHAPTER 3

A New People

The foregoing indicates that progressive scientists will continuously have to face the issues of racism and racial violence, but the main purpose of this book is not in this area. Here, we are primarily concerned with the living examples and with peoples' experiences of what happens when an environment undergoes change.

What has taken place in the German Democratic Republic in almost a quarter of a century of existence will engage the attention and evoke the admiration of generations to come. For, what has been done there against the background of the most difficult conditions is one of the "miracles" of our time.

For the last 15 or 20 years, the bourgeoisie in the Western world, and the United States in particular, have spent billions of dollars trying to distort the image of the people who built a new state, the German Democratic Republic. They spent billions trying to make West Germany a showcase for capitalist and imperialist policies. That was the real meaning of the Marshall Plan. They spent additional millions organizing a network of propaganda agencies directed toward the people of East Germany about the "democratic" and superior way of life in West Germany. The monopoly-dominated press in almost all countries of the Western world had daily distorted everything taking place inside East Germany, trying to make it appear as a slave camp.

But now the chickens have come home to roost. The achievements of the people of the G.D.R. are so tremendous that the bourgeoisie finds it necessary to admit the truth, while still trying to distort their meaning.

Almost everyone who goes to the G.D.R. today comes back to their countries so favorably impressed that even the bourgeois press has to take note:

From the newspaper *Nieuwe Linie*, Amsterdam, June 5, 1965:

> "It is now apparent that the image we have gradually built up in our minds about this country (the G.D.R.) is completely archaic. East Berlin has also become an open city where foreigners are gladly and hospitably received. One can experience for oneself, in daily life, that East Germany has really become the eighth industrial country in the world. That one can even speak of a 'small economic miracle' . . ."

Hans Hammers, in *De Groene Amsterdammer*, Amsterdam, June 24, 1967, wrote:

> "Recently, a delegation of Amsterdam journalists travelled informally to East Berlin at the invitation of the journalists' association there . . . I came back frightened. Frightened, because I can now understand, for the first time, how great the gulf is between the reality in the G.D.R. and the picture we have been given of it in our land.

And that, despite the fact that the G.D.R. is a state that occupies a key position in the over-all political development of Europe.

"For most Netherlands citizens the G.D.R. is a white area on the map, a sort of Siberian 'no man's land' which terrorizes its inhabitants in order to force them to accept their bad standard of living . . . That the G.D.R. is a state that the irrefutable statistics of growth show to have attained a solid material and intellectual pros-perity is understood by only a few . . . And how many know that a multi-party system exists, and also functions? Who has grasped the practical ideology behind its cultural and press policy? Who is informed about the aims and the un-folding of its planned economy, about the development of its agriculture? How do things stand, for example, with the reconstruction, say, of Dresden, with the education system, with the cost of living?

"These are questions to which only an ex-ceptionally small group of people in our country know the answers. Our newspapers, of course, have correspondents in the Federal Republic. But not a single newspaper receives regular in-formation from the G.D.R. The far greatest por-tion of the information about the G.D.R. that reaches the average Netherlands citizen comes from West German sources. This information is completely coloured by the political struggles be-tween the two Germanys . . ."

*

One of the organs of the French bourgeoisie, *Le Monde Diplomatique*, Paris, December, 1967, observed:

> "... The German Democratic Republic exists. To refuse to recognize it officially is just as senseless as the refusal to recognize the Oder-Neisse border. That is valid for the Federal Republic, whose attempts to court the East will remain blocked as long as it refuses to recognize the fact of the G.D.R. ..."

These examples of impressions from people who have gone to the G.D.R. reflect a new stage in the history of the new German state. Regarding these achievements, a large number of books in the English language have recently appeared in which the economic achievements of the G.D.R. are well documented. They all make the point that West Germany, which was the more prosperous of the two German states in the immediate postwar years, has now lost ground to the G.D.R.

But three things characterize most of these books and writers: Notwithstanding the positive assessments they contain, most of them still seek to cover up the substance behind the achievements. On the other hand, there are those who say that the economic achievements in the G.D.R. came in spite of its powerful allies. In other words, what has been achieved in the G.D.R. has no relation to the socialist community in general, nor to the Soviet Union in particular.

Another aspect of these commentaries on the

G.D.R. is the fact that few writers properly assess the achievement of the people in the G.D.R. in eradicating racism from their midst. Most writers who have discussed the G.D.R. (including many progressives and people of good will) have not taken note of these achievements. It is almost as if they meant to say that the problem of racism never existed, or that, if it has been solved, it is a secondary matter.

Yes, the people of the German Democratic Republic have eradicated racism in their country, and in so doing have once again given to the world proof that racism is not inherent in man. This phenomenon came about and flourished in the context of changes in the entire social, economic and political environment of people.

It is in this respect—the building of a socialist society—that the people of the G.D.R. have made their magnificent contribution. It is not only an example of ending racism in their own country, but they also provide an answer to what is required all over the world to end racism. The socialist community they have built is based on the concepts expounded by Leonid Brezhnev at the Lenin Centenary Celebration, where he stated:

> "One of the greatest achievements of socialism is that every Soviet citizen is assured of his future. He is aware that his work, his abilities and his energy will always find a fitting use and appreciation. He is sure that his children will be given a free education and the possibility of developing their talents. He knows that society

will never abandon him in misfortune, that in the event of illness he will be given free medical treatment, a pension in the event of permanent disability, and security in old age."

What Breshnev says here about the Soviet Union is likewise true about the German Democratic Republic. Every citizen of the G.D.R. knows that society will never abandon him in misfortune. When I was there in the summer of 1970, I had an interview with one of the pensioners who had left the G.D.R. to live in West Germany. She had children in West Germany and felt that the economic conditions there were much better, and she left for these reasons. A few years later she returned to live in the German Democratic Republic. When asked why, she replied, "Over there (meaning West Germany), everybody is on his own. Over here (meaning the G.D.R.) nobody is alone." In these few simple words, a whole world is conveyed. The message was: Under capitalism everybody is out for himself, while under socialism, all are concerned about each other and whatever the fortunes –good or bad–the community shares the problems of the individual.

When I returned home I found that the views of this woman had become a general phenomenon. *Newsweek*, one of America's most influential and widely circulated magazines, in its September 14, 1970 issue, commented as follows:

"Before the Berlin wall went up in 1961, 3.5 million Germans fled from East to West, seeking the promised land of political freedom and economic opportunity. Little has been heard of them since, and the world has generally assumed that they were happily assimilated into Western society. Yet in the past decade, half a million disillusioned refugees have returned to East Germany. And of those who stayed on in West Germany, many still harbor a nostalgic fascination for the collective life of a Communist state."

These observations were based on a book written by Barbara-Grunert-Bronnen, titled *I'm a Citizen of the G.D.R. and live in the Federal Republic*, (Pieper-Verlag Munich, 1970). Mrs. Bronnen had had interviews with people who had left the G.D.R. in previous years.

Newsweek sent a team of reporters to the Federal Republic to check the accuracy of Mrs. Bronnen's report. They confirmed her findings. Among their comments were:

"'Freedom is fine,' said one refugee, 'but it has its pitfalls, too ... People are only concerned with themselves here.' And a housewife added: 'The sense of being needed by the community and the willingness to serve it was much stronger in the East. I was far from being a backer of the party's goals–I wasn't even in the party–but I gladly performed community functions in my free time that I wouldn't dream of doing here. Besides, no one has asked me to do anything.'" (Ibid.)

Finally, these reporters from *Newsweek* summed up the situation as follows:

"Apart from such 'atmospherics,' the refugees list concrete advantages for life under socialism: better hospitals, more homes for the aged, a more comprehensive medical insurance system. 'The retirement payments are admittedly low, but there's no retired person in the G.D.R. going hungry, as is the case here,' remarked a 38-year-old engineer. And all the refugees interviewed by Mrs. Gruner-Bronnen—as well as those *Newsweek* interviewed in an attempt to check her findings—agreed that East Germany's educational system is superior to that in the West. 'Particularly languages and physics—are all much better,' said an artist who studied in Leipzig. 'Socialist education,' said a woman from Pomerania, 'teaches a sensitivity towards injustice.' In the G.D.R., say refugees, people are more critical, both of their own country and of West Germany.

"The insights offered by Mrs. Grunert-Bronnen have aroused considerable comment in West Germany. In an unusual four-column review in the *Frankfurter Allgemeine Zeitung*, West German novelist Magret Boveri admitted: 'We in the Federal Republic are held up to a mirror which no longer, or at least only in certain cases, makes of us the fairest land.' Novelist Uwe Johnson, who wrote a sensitive epilogue to the interviews, pointed out that 'the G.D.R., as teacher, regardless of how harshly and whimsically it went about things, could for a long time draw its unquestioned authority from the twin moral roots of anti-Fascism and the new social order. In these interviews the G.D.R. emerges almost as a sort of personality—while the Federal Republic is nothing except the place where one happens to be.' "

(Ibid.)

It is evident from these developments that a new human being is being created in the G.D.R.—a socialist man—and if there is anything that characterizes this new man it is his understanding that he is "his brother's keeper." What theologians talked about for centuries, the people of the G.D.R. have put into practice. This new man is in direct contrast to the kind of person bred by the insecurity of capitalism, a society which thrives on "dog-eat-dog" a system that supports everything selfish in man.

As indicated, capitalism came into the world and advanced mankind to better technology and higher scientific achievements, but in human relations it will quit the stage of history as the most corrupt and immoral system ever devised by the mind of man.

Karl Marx scathingly denounced the capitalist order and described its nature with great clarity when he wrote:

"The bourgeoisie has stripped of its halo every occupation hitherto honored and looked up to with reverent awe. It has converted the physician, the lawyer, the priest, the poet, the man of science, into its paid wage laborers.

"The bourgeoisie has torn away from the family its sentimental veil, and has reduced the family relation to a mere money relation."

(Karl Marx, *Communist Manifesto*, International Publishers, New York, 1948, p. 11.)

Capitalism glorifies those who rise at the expense of their brothers and denounces as being backward those who do not achieve this "distinction." Success is measured by how much money a man acquires. Principles, morals and character mean nothing.

The people in the G.D.R., having transformed their mentality to that of a community concerned about the welfare of the man next door, in the next block, in its city, in its country and in the world, has laid the basis upon which a new nation has come on to the world scene, a nation no longer practicing racism. In doing this, the people in the German Democratic Republic have made a profound contribution to the advancement of all mankind.

But in order fully to appreciate this success, to understand it and to apply its lessons to concrete experiences and circumstances wherever people are in struggle against monopoly capitalism and imperialism, it is necessary to know how this magnificent achievement was organized and carried out.

CHAPTER 4

The Source from which
a New People Developed

The people of the German Democratic Republic went through a long and difficult process before they emerged as a force which has made significant achievements. History records few examples of a people having had to start anew with a legacy such as the G.D.R. inherited from the twelve years of Nazi rule. A study of this background and their achievements shows that the environmental factor is the dominant force promoting racism and war. A study of its history in the last quarter century illuminates the path to building a world based on peace, freedom and equality.

On May 8, 1945, the most horrible war in history ended with the defeat of the Nazi war machine. The war transformed much of Europe and also parts of Asia and Africa into scorched earth. There were 23 million dead soldiers and 35 million wounded. It cost trillions of dollars. The U.S.S.R. alone had 20,300,000 dead. It bore the main burden of the struggle against Hitlerite Germany. Poland had 6 million dead, and Yugoslavia 1,700,000, France counted over 600,000, the United States about 400,000, and Great Britain over 375,000 killed. Eleven million people were murdered in concentration camps.

Due to the criminal activities of the Nazi war lords, to the fact that millions of Germans were blinded by Hitler and became instrumental in bringing such destruction to the world, the German people themselves paid an awful price, some 8 million dead. Thirty-six million were wounded and crippled. Hardly a town escaped without destruction. Almost every family left mourned the loss of one or more members or close relatives. The people were plunged into unbelievable misery, suffering hunger and poverty. This was the price paid for supporting the fascist and racist politics of the fascist politicians and military men.

After the war there were still greater problems. Most of the people were in despair. Their world had caved in on them.

It is against this background that the achievements of the German Democratic Republic must be evaluated. Of key importance is an understanding of the social forces. The circumstances which enabled the people of the G.D.R. to triumph over the terrible conditions mentioned above are rooted in social processes that today are world-wide in scope. In general, these begin with the emergence of the scientific concepts of Socialism formulated and developed by Marx, Engels and Lenin. They are rooted in the lessons drawn from the disasters that befell the international working class movement owing to the betrayal by the Social-Democratic leaders during and after World War I, not least in Germany. They are rooted in the October Revolution in Czarist Russia in 1917. They emerge out of the concept established by Karl Marx– "Workers of the World Unite; You have nothing to lose but your chains!" They are part and parcel of the

Marxist principle that a "nation which oppresses another cannot, itself, be free." They are based upon the concept of proletarian internationalism, carried forward by Lenin and the Bolsheviks in 1917.

In an assessment of social phenomena, one must look for the pathfinders, the people who are conscious of what has to be done, the people who are capable of making the sacrifices required to change an existing state of affairs.

What was the situation in the Eastern zone of Germany, the Soviet-occupied zone, at war's end in 1945? Where did the people come from who undertook to take a lead in undoing the damage caused by Hitler's rule?

These people came primarily from the ranks of the German anti-fascists who fought Hitler in the concentration camps and in all walks of life, when detection meant death. It is estimated that the fascist regime, on its way to the destruction of a large portion of Europe, brought death to 500,000 anti-fascists within the country. But even a Hitler could not destroy all the anti-fascist forces. Many fighters stayed inside Germany and continued their struggle there; others went to other countries to organize resistance that aided materially in the ultimate defeat of the fascist forces. A comprehensive history of the heroism of the German anti-fascists is still to be written. They represented people of many persuasions, but the decisive force among them was the German Communist Party.

This party was born in struggle against the chauvinism of the right-wing leaders of the Social-Democratic Party who, in World War I, had supported their own imperialist government. It was composed of that sector of the Social-Democratic Party which had defied Kaiser Wilhelm's government and the war aims of German imperialism. Inspired by the ideals of the Russian Revolution of 1917, it was founded two years after that revolution by Karl Liebknecht and Rosa Luxemburg. The German Communist Party, from the very first days of the threat of German fascism and a new war, warned of these dangers. On November 24, 1925, Ernst Thaelmann, the leader of the party, arose in the German Reichstag and proclaimed:

> "The hearts of the military among German re-action are already beginning to beat more quickly. German reaction is already dreaming of starting with the mopping up of their 'sworn enemies,' the Poles. We must now show the true nature of the German bourgeoisie's eastern policy to the German and the international working class. What the German bourgeoisie is here quietly organizing can tomorrow become an enormous, bloody adventure . . ."
>
> (From *Alliance With the Future*, Verlag Zeit im Bild, Dresden, 1969, p. 14.)

Throughout the entire period of post-World War I developments, the Communist Party of Germany was advancing a program which could have saved the nation and the world from having to pass through the horrors of the twelve years of Hitler's rule. The German Communists did not avoid making some mistakes, which they themselves have admitted, but their mistakes were mainly of tactical nature and not fundamental.

A factor of supreme importance for the struggle of German anti-fascists was the role of the U.S.S.R. The aid given to the anti-fascist movement, not only in the pre-war period but during World War II by the Soviet people, was one of the greatest acts of friendship between peoples in history. Soviet aid to the German anti-fascist cause during World War II was invaluable —and it was given in full view of the vast losses and destruction such as took place during the siege of Leningrad, in which over a million men, women and children died. All along the battle fronts, wherever the Nazi army marched, they wantonly murdered the civilian population. Millions of Soviet citizens were driven off to slave labor camps and to the ammunition plants of the Krupps and the Thyssens. In the face of brutality unsurpassed in all of human history, the Soviet people, under the guidance and leadership of the Communist Party of the Soviet Union, never lost their perspective and their ideal of proletarian internationalism.

In 1943 a Free German National Committee was set up. It was composed of leading Communists, Social-Democrats and liberals, as well as Christian priests and included some German army officers such as Field Marshal Paulus, who had commanded the assault on Stalingrad. Representatives of this Committee conducted classes among the prisoners of war in the Soviet Union and appealed to the German people not to support the Nazi war machine.

The respect for and confidence in the German working class and its socialist-minded people by the Soviet people were rooted in many facts of history. There is a tradition of mutual support by the workers of Germany and the Soviet Union in the struggle against a common enemy. German workers played a role in helping in the success of the October Revolution in 1917. Let us cite the case of a German metal worker who was in a Russian prisoner of war camp at the time of the October Revolution. He wrote:

> ". . . At the time of the October Revolution I was in Central Asia. The October Revolution was my revolution, the revolution of my class, of all the oppressed and exploited. Its defense I recognised as a just war; its final victory signified for me, too, the first step, towards the victory of socialism throughout the world."
>
> (Hans Zebrowske, "I Was a Special Red Army Courier in Central Asia," in *Weltenwende*, Dietz Verlag, Berlin, 1962, p. 284.)

There were many similar expressions of support of the October Revolution by German workers, and participation as well.

I pride myself on having been a student of the history of the Bolshevik Revolution. However, I discovered I did not know some of the details. I knew that Lenin, at the turn of the century, had organized an illegal newspaper called *Iskra*, which had been instrumental in welding together the socialist forces in Czarist Russia. But I did not know that Lenin had gone to Germany where socialists had helped him to put the paper out. On a recent trip to the G.D.R., I visited the printing plant in a suburb just outside of Leipzig. As I walked around the plant and learned of the support he had received in Germany, I better understood the friendship between the Russian and German workers which could withstand wartime devastation and the atrocities of German fascists.

Thus, the friendship of Russian and German workers in the past, the principle of proletarian internationalism, made possible Soviet aid for an anti-fascist force capable of re-organizing the German people for constructive purposes.

Shortly before the war ended, a program was advanced from the Soviet sector of the battle front by the Free German National Committee which called for "... the creation of a strong democratic power, the complete revocation of all laws based on national and racial hatred, and the restitution and extension of the political rights and social achievents of the working people."

It called for the immediate liberation of the victims of fascist terror and material compensation for the injury they had suffered, and the relentless and just punishment of those who were responsible for the war. The U.S.S.R. consulted with German anti-fascists and helped them publicize their plans.

The Communist Party of Germany, a few months before the Potsdam Agreement was signed, came forward with a program similar to that agreed on at Potsdam. On June 11, 1945, it set forth the strategy and tactics that later became the guiding line for the Eastern zone of Germany. The CP stated:

"Now it is a question of learning the lessons of the past thoroughly and forever. We must enter upon an entirely new road!

"May every German become aware of the fact that the road taken by our people up to now was a false road which led to guilt and disgrace, war and ruin!

"Not only the rubble of the destroyed towns, but the reactionary rubble of the past must be thoroughly removed. May the reconstruction of Germany take place on a solid basis so that a third repetition of the imperialist policy of catastrophe is impossible.

"The destruction of Hitlerism is also a question of completing the democratization of Germany, the bourgeois-democratic revolution which began in 1848, of completely removing the feudal vestiges and destroying old Prussian militarism with its economic and political offshoots.

"We believe that forcing the Soviet system on Germany would be wrong, for this way does not correspond to the present conditions of development.

"We rather think the decisive interests of the German people at present prescribe another way, the setting up of an anti-fascist, democratic regime, a parliamentary-democratic republic with all democratic rights and liberties.

"At the present historical turning point, we Communists call all working people, all democratic and progressive forces to this great struggle for

the democratic renewal of Germany, for the re-
birth of our country!"

(From *Way and Goal of the German People*,
Tenth Anniversary of the Founding of the
G.D.R., September 1959, p. 24.)

In August 1945 the Potsdam Agreement was concluded by the U.S.A., Great Britain and the U.S.S.R.
Among other things, the Potsdam Agreement provided:

III. Germany
*... German militarism and Nazism will be extir-
pated ... to assure that Germany will never again
threaten her neighbors or the peace of the world.*

A. Political Principles
*3. III. To destroy the National Socialist Party and its
affiliated and supervised organizations, to dissolve all
Nazi institutions, to ensure that they are not revived
in any form, and to prevent all Nazi and militarist
activity or propaganda.*

*5. War criminals and those who have participated in
planning or carrying out Nazi enterprises involving
or resulting in atrocities or war crimes shall be arrested
and brought to judgment. Nazi leaders, influential
Nazi supporters ... and any other persons dangerous
to the occupation or its objectives shall be arrested
and interned.*

*6. All members of the Nazi party who have been more
than nominal participants in its activities, and all
other persons hostile to allied purposes, shall be removed from public and semi-public office, and from*

*positions of responsibility in important private under-
takings. Such persons shall be replaced by persons
who, by their political and moral qualities, are deemed
capable of assisting in developing genuine democratic
institutions in Germany.*

B. Economic Principles
*12. At the earliest practicable date, the German econ-
omy shall be decentralized for the purpose of eliminating the present excessive concentration of economic
power as exemplified in particular by cartels, syndicates, trusts and other monopolistic arrangements.*

With this program from the Potsdam Agreement in
the background, the Communist Party of Germany
determined to implement the policy outlined as quickly
as possible. It brought with it a broader vision of what
had to be done than had existed in the pre-Hitler period. Its concepts of the scope of the alliances required
resulted from painful experience. Many members of
the Social-Democratic Party who had refused to cooperate with the Communist Party in the pre-Hitler
period, had likewise learned the need to overcome
anti-Communist prejudices.

The first prerequisite was the unity of the working
class. Such unity required unity of the party representing that class, under whose leadership the workers
could proceed with peaceful reconstruction. So, on
April 22, 1946, 507 Communist and 548 Social-Democratic delegates decided at a Congress to unite the
two parties and found the Socialist Unity Party of
Germany (SED), led by Wilhelm Pieck and Walter
Ulbricht, veteran leaders of the Communist Party,

and Otto Grotewohl and Friedrich Ebert Jr., leaders of the Social-Democrats. Some months earlier the Confederation of Free German Trade Unions had been established, thereby laying the basis for complete unity of the working class.

The new party developed an approach which called for an alliance of the working class with other strata of the population. Thus, from the very beginning, a coalition policy with other classes and parties was established by the SED. A bloc agreement was concluded with the Christian Democratic Union Party and the Liberal Democratic Party, both founded in 1945. Later, a Peasant Party also joined. In 1948, this democratic bloc was enlarged by the newly founded National Democratic Party of Germany, consisting mainly of former soldiers and officers and disillusioned followers of Hitler who had not held positions of any importance under fascist rule, and wished actively to support democratic reconstruction.

These events were mainly the work of the older generation of anti-fascist fighters. Now, based upon this solid foundation of anti-fascist forces and unity of the working class, an effort was made to enlist the younger generation between the ages of 13 and 20. The youth, indoctrinated in fascism under Hitler, had seen the world of its beliefs collapse beyond repair. They were young and it was, in many cases, not too difficult to undo the harm done to them. Thus, the two generations met and became the force to put the house in order in the Soviet-occupied zone of Germany. Today, twenty-seven years later, men and women in their early forties in great numbers do responsible work at all levels of government, politics and economy.

Between 1948-49, the Confederation of Free German Trade Unions, the Free German Youth, the Democratic Women's Federation of Germany, the German League of Culture, together with the political parties, established the National Front of Democratic Germany. These were the forces that organized and carried through the provisions of the Potsdam Agreement in the Eastern Zone. One of its first acts centered around Point No. 7 of the June 11, 1945 Appeal of the German Communist Party. It called for:

> "Liquidation of the large landed property, the large estates of Junkers, counts and princes and distribution of all their land to farmers who were ruined and rendered destitute by the war."

In this act were summed up centuries of history. As far back as 1525, peasants had waged tremendous struggles for land. However, not having the support of the emerging young bourgeois in the cities, the peasants were defeated, their leaders tortured, broken on the wheel and beheaded. Historians say that the defeated peasants sang in defiance—"Our heirs will do a better job!"

It took 420 years before these heirs came to do the job. Statistics for the year 1933 show that 34,000 large landowners had 35,200,000 acres, while a million small farmers owned only 7,480,000. The majority of higher officials and nearly the whole officer corps of Prussia came from the small social group of wealthy landlords.

In 1945, when the Land Reform began, it received a great response. Farm workers and small holders elected over 52,000 people into the local Land Reform Commissions. The law provided that landed property of active Nazis and war criminals, as well as any piece of property over 220 acres, was to be expropriated without compensation, and distributed to farm workers, poor peasants and settlers. Altogether, 7,255,780 acres (35 percent of the area under cultivation) were transferred to the land fund. On this fund 4,817,998 acres were distributed to 559,089 applicants, including 119,121 landless peasants and farm workers, as well as 91,155 resettled families.

Changing ownership was only a first step. Now it was necessary to provide homes for the new owners.

So the industrial workers took up a "second job"— salvaging bricks from the ruins of their bombed cities for the villages. On Sundays, bricklayers and carpenters worked at such building. By 1953, over 95,000 homes and 142,500 farm buildings had been constructed. For this, the new state provided very generous credits at favorable rates of interest. Over half of these credits were later remitted.

As a complement to the Land Reform, steps were taken to break the power of the monopolies in industry and finance, whose elimination the Potsdam Agreement had called for. This process began on June 30, 1946 with a plebiscite in Saxony, the most highly developed industrial area in the Eastern Zone. This plebiscite called for the expropriation of the properties of war and Nazi criminals.

Many meetings and public demands showed that

large parts of the population considered the referendum a day of judgment of the people. On this question the workers were of one mind with the small scale farmers, tradesmen, resettlers, intellectuals, clergymen and former rank and file members of the Nazi party. The trade unionists in Dresden, for example, declared:

> "This general meeting of shop committee members and trade union officials of the Dresden region of the Confederation of Free German Trade Unions unanimously demands the transfer of the enterprises of war and Nazi criminals to the democratic organs of self-administration. They demand this to ensure the peaceful development of the economy. They thereby wish to pave the way for a better future for the working sections of Germany and prove to the world that the democratic forces have taken over the leadership and that those guilty of the Hitler crimes and the war will be punished."

The echo in the population showed that the SED had assessed the situation correctly in its appeal for the referendum. Saxony set an example: In the vote on June 30, 1946, the anti-fascist forces won an outstanding victory; 94.1 percent of the people had made use of their right to vote; 77.7 percent said "Yes" to this vital question: 5.8 percent of the votes were invalid, and only 16.5 percent defended the war criminals. This was an unambiguous judgment of the majority of the population regarding the war criminals and profiteers.

The poll in Saxony proved that the relation of

forces in East Germany had significantly changed in favor of the anti-fascist, democratic forces. Their unity formed the cornerstone of the policies of the SED. The large participation in the voting and the positive vote of 77.7 percent proved that the people were with those who wished to safeguard the democratic development of Germany.

Even before the plebiscite in Saxony, large sections of the public in the Soviet occupation zone had declared for the referendum. Decrees on the taking over of the enterprises of war criminals and their transfer to the people were enacted in Thuringia, Saxony-Anhalt, Brandenburg and Mecklenburg, in July and August of 1946. In the provincial bodies, the representatives of the working class, the peasants and the middle classes agreed upon regulations for the expropriation, which was later carried through by the workers in alliance with the democratic members of other sections of the population.

Perhaps the most difficult job was to implement the decisions of the Potsdam Conference on school reform. There were many problems, such as the lack of trained personnel capable of coping with academic problems. Nonetheless, the anti-fascists did not shirk these problems. The resumption of school instruction on October 1, 1945 was preceded by a great deal of work. First was the removal of those teachers who had been Nazis. Of 37,000 teachers in the territory that is now the G.D.R., 22,600 had been Nazi Party members and had to be dismissed. Some argued against this on the grounds that the teaching standard of the schools would be impaired: but the anti-fascist forces remained firm, being more concerned with the content than with the form. They correctly believed that the new teaching staffs would, in time, become fully competent in every respect.

By the end of 1945, 45,244 new teachers, mostly coming from the working class, had been trained. They set about educating young people to be independent-thinking citizens, conscious of their task of building a new democratic and anti-fascist state. All chauvinist, racist and colonialist thinking was to be eliminated. The task given to the new school system was to promote and consolidate the democratic unity of the nation. Almost as difficult as training a competent teaching staff was the problem of devising the curriculum and designing new textbooks.

The Land Reform, the expropriation of the monopolies and trusts which had without exception belonged to war criminals, denazification of all areas of public life, elimination of former Nazis from public responsibilities, democratic school reform, as well as strengthening the anti-fascist-democratic coalition, were the foundations upon which the new house was built.

CHAPTER 5

An Economic "Miracle"

The economic achievements of the German Democratic Republic have won acclaim throughout the world. Many refer to them as an economic miracle, and when the background is considered on which these results were arrived at it is no wonder they are considered astounding.

At the war's end, the Eastern zone of Germany, now known as the G.D.R., inherited most unfavorable conditions for its growth and development. Firstly, it comprised the smaller part of Germany, with a population of about 17 millions and no seaport of any significance. It had few of the raw materials required for industrialization. Compared with the larger (western) part of Germany, the disproportion in natural resources is striking. Pre-war East Germany produced less than one percent of the country's coke, less than 3 percent of its hard coal, less than 5 percent of its iron ore and less than 7 percent of its finished steel products. These disproportions in respect to the resources needed for industrialization tell only part of the story.

In addition, the destruction caused by the war was far greater in the east. It was in this area that the Nazi leaders and generals at the end resorted increasingly to a scorched-earth policy. Hitler's war machine did all it could to retard the entry into Germany of the

Red Army. It was more prepared to accept the occupation by the allied powers than by the Soviet Union. It is estimated that the destruction of industry in the eastern part of Germany reached a level of 45 percent (in machine building, of 70 percent), in comparison with a mere 20 percent in the western part. Moreover, there was enormous destruction in transport, in the cities and in agriculture, due to indiscriminate bombing in the last period of the war. The United States greatly stepped up its bombing operations in order to desolate that area before the Red Army occupied it.

The destruction of urban housing and of livestock was especially heavy in the eastern part of Germany. The country as a whole suffered 35 percent destruction of urban housing, but in the eastern section, it was 50 percent. In the territory later occupied by the Soviet Union, 30 percent of all agricultural machinery was destroyed; the number of cattle dropped to 65.7 percent of pre-war levels, and that of hogs to 20.7 percent.*

In addition to such economic disproportions, the G.D.R. entered the postwar world with a world-wide boycott against it by the major capitalist powers. Through such projects as the Marshall Plan, West Germany was enabled to recuperate much faster than was the Eastern zone. The Soviet Union, which had borne the brunt of the war, did not have the same immediate capacity to aid the East. Consequently, living standards in the West were at first considerably

* Figures from article "Economic Miracle: G.D.R.", by Muller and Reisig, Berlin, 1968, p. 15.

higher than in the East—a fact which led quite a few people to move westwards, thereby increasing difficulties in Eastern economy.

All these factors badly handicapped the people of the G.D.R. in beginning the process of reconstruction. Notwithstanding the difficulties, certain fundamental factors opened up possibilities for an unprecedented growth of the economy. According to the pamphlet, *The Anti-Fascist State*, the economic successes were possible

> ". . . because, thanks to the intelligent economic policy of the SED, a strong, constantly growing, nationally owned sector of the economy was set up early. In the nationally-owned enterprises the working people were for the first time in German history not working for the prosperity of individuals, but for themselves, for the community. The knowledge that they owned the means of production brought about a basic change in the workers' attitude toward their work and gave them the strength to achieve pioneering performances."
>
> (Dresden, 1969, p. 31.)

That is to say, the achievements were due to the transformation of the social system to socialism in the 'fifties. However, most commentators in capitalist countries cannot face up to this fact. Hence, their characterization of the economic successes of the G.D.R. as a "miracle". In reality the achievements demonstrate the superiority of socialism over capitalism.

Developments also show that it is possible for a people to attain an increasingly high standard of living without exploiting other peoples. Hitler's temporary economic successes resulted largely from the exploitation of other countries. The high rate and level of development of the capitalist powers in the past was partly based upon robbery of the colonial peoples throughout the world.

The economic growth was achieved under great difficulties. Nonetheless, from the beginning its economy evinced a continuous growth. Between 1946 and 1950, pre-war levels were reached, and then began its first Five Year Plan.

Year after year, despite all obstacles, the economy of the G.D.R. grew in strength. Industrial production rose steadily; economic cooperation with the other socialist countries, and particularly with the Soviet Union, became closer; new experts, a high proportion of them from the working class, brought a new quality into the planning and management of a socialist economy. At the same time, in the countryside the farmers were coming together in cooperatives, pooling their fields so that they could be worked more efficiently with the modern agricultural machinery becoming available.

One serious difficulty, which was a drag on the economy for many years was the "open frontier" between the G.D.R. and West Berlin. By means of smuggling, currency manipulation, and the luring away of skilled workers to jobs in West Germany, the imperialists damaged the G.D.R. to the tune of hundreds of millions of dollars. This drain on the economy was brought to an end on August 13, 1961 when, on the decision of the powers of the Warsaw Pact, the open frontier between the G.D.R. and West Berlin became passable only for those persons with the prescribed passports, visas, etc.

Early in 1963, at its Sixth Congress, the Socialist Unity Party could state that conditions were ripe for a qualitatively new type of economic and social development. That summer, the new system of economic planning and management was introduced. Its chief elements were:

1. Central planning which aims at a broad perspective (to about 1975) for production and trade turnover.

2. Scientific management of enterprises. As a decisive measure to this end, Associations of Nationally-Owned Enterprises (numbering about 80) were made the leading organs responsible for the profitability of the industrial branches.

3. The most varied participation of the working people in the direct planning and management of the enterprises and of the national economy and the state. The forms of socialist democracy extend from production conferences, in which management and workers submit proposals, to deliberations on tasks planned for the following year.

4. The interest of individual workers in the results of production is encouraged; those who help create additional values receive greater material acknowledgement.

Together with the new economic system, an industrial price reform was carried out in three stages, from 1964 to 1967. It was necessary to create a basic relationship between prices and socially necessary costs. The price reform obliges enterprises to rationalize economic management (economize on raw and auxiliary materials), in order to earn as much profit as possible. From this, the workers also benefit.

The first stage of the new economic system (1963–1965) was followed by a second stage in 1966. The aim is to increase the gross product and secure a maximum growth of national income and its most effective utilization. This primarily requires strengthening scientific planning, a task for which the employment of modern data-processing is needed. The G.D.R. concentrates all its forces on bringing its economy into line with the requirements of the scientific-technical revolution, which is aimed at speedily increasing the wealth of the people.

The new economic system continues to develop the country's economy successfully and, after only a few years, has already achieved good results.

Industrial production in 1967 totaled about 150 billion marks (in 1961 it had been 107 billion), a gain of over 40 percent in six years. National income rose by 14 billion marks between 1962 and 1966. During this period, labor productivity grew by 24 percent.

During this period the G.D.R., though with a population of only 17 millions, developed into one of the ten leading industrial nations of the world and ranked fifth in Europe. Its growth was phenomenal in almost all industries, but outstandingly so in chemicals. This profoundly affected the entire economy. Today, this industry per capita, is second only to that of the United States. Taking 100 as an index of petroleum production in 1962, within six years it rose to about 900. Between 1965 and 1970, the following results were registered:

The basic tasks of the Five Year Plan (1966–70) were fulfilled and, in some cases, overfulfilled.

The *national income* grew from 84 billion marks in 1965 to 108 billion by 1970, a gain of 29 percent, or an annual growth rate of 5.2 percent.

Investments increased from 20.5 billion marks in 1965 to 32.6 billion in 1970, or a total of 59 percent. Those in industry grew by 51 percent during that period. Investments in the total national economy between 1966 and 1970 were 127.4 billion marks. Actually, 135.6 billion were invested. The sum fixed for industry in the 1966–70 Plan was exceeded by 3 percent.

Industrial production grew by 37 percent from 1966 to 1970. That means that the objectives of the Five Year Plan were achieved. The increase in production was, above all, due to a growth in labor productivity (33 percent), particularly in the branches of the economy determining technological progress.

Electrical engineering, electronics and scientific instrument output grew by 61 percent, reaching the highest rate of industrial development.

Chemical output in 1970 grew by 50 percent as against that of 1965, and increased its share in total industrial production to 16 percent. In past years, considerable means were employed from the G.D.R.'s own resources for construction in petro-chemistry, as well as for prospecting, extracting and use of natural gas. Synthetic fibers output has more than doubled, and that of plastics increased by 75 percent.

The *building industry* increased output by 48 percent from 1965 to 1970. Light metal construction with a considerable capacity was developed in the course of two years. In industrial and housing construction, as well as in the building of schools and institutions for children, not all goals were reached.

In *agriculture*, the aims of the Five Year Plan have been surpassed in meat packing, poultry and egg output. Market production of animal products per acre of arable land increased by 20 percent. The aims set by the Plan could not be achieved for grains and milk, due to bad weather in 1969 and 1970.

Retail trade turnover was in 1970 25 percent higher than in 1965. Half of all households now have washing machines and refrigerators. As to television sets, the figure is 70 percent. However, services and repairs have lagged behind.*

Based upon these solid achievements, the people of the G.D.R. have worked out plans for an accelerated growth rate in almost every area. The main task of the 1971–75 Plan is to raise further the material and cultural living standards of the people, on the basis of increased effectiveness in scientific and technological progress and a growth in labor productivity. The Plan envisions:

- A rise in national income by 27 percent.
- Industrial goods production to be increased 34 percent.

* As reported at the VIII Congress of the SED, June 1971.

- Labor productivity of workers and employees in industry to increase 35 percent.
- Consumption to increase 22 percent. The real income of the population to increase 22 percent on this basis.
- Total investments in the national economy to increase by 29 percent compared to the 1966–1970 period.

The Plan now under way does not envisage an accelerated building of new plants. The problem is how better to utilize existing facilities and, above all, to increase labor productivity. This goal is to be achieved through a technological revolution, automations and increased skill of labor.

The scientific and technological revolution in the capitalist world is creating untold problems—dislocation of jobs, deterioration in conditions of the working people, etc.—because of the nature of the system whose primary concern is profit-making. In the G.D.R., this is no problem. The working class assists the government in carrying out the objectives of rationalization in industry. They do so because they can face the future with confidence that the new technology and scientific methods will create a more wholesome life for the average worker. This confidence is derived from experience.

Progressively, as the economy has grown, the standard of living and services to the people have correspondingly increased. From 1950 to 1963, real wages went up 3.5 times, while prices declined, with a corresponding rise in purchasing power.

This has of course meant a considerable all-round

improvement in the conditions of the workers and farmers. In 1967, the five-day work week was established. Working women have been helped by the establishment of pre-school and all-day educational establishments. The following chart illustrates this progress:

Year	Places in crèches and homes	In Kindergartens and homes	Pupils in all-day educational institutions
1955	59.3	308.9	116.1
1960	92.4	405.3	299.4
1965	126.3	511.0	424.3
1968	153.8	580.1	502.6
1970	174.2	620.1	575.6

With respect to consumer goods per 100 households, the following table reveals the increases:

Year	Automobiles	Television sets	Refrigerators	Washing machines
1955	0.2	1.2	0.4	0.5
1960	3.2	16.7	6.1	6.2
1964	7.1	42.2	20.4	22.4
1968	12.2	65.0	43.9	43.1
1970	15.3	69.1	56.4	53.7

The G.D.R., overall, plans not only for increases per capita in income, but it also provides for many other services contributing to the general well-being.

Take the question of housing. To organize socialist

housing, more community facilities were created in new residential areas. The number of places in schools and other institutions for children per 100 apartments was raised from 75 in 1966 to 110 four years later. Housing construction became an increasingly important aspect of the organization of city centers. During a visit to the G.D.R. in early 1971, I toured Leipzig with the person in charge of housing construction and he explained to me how new buildings had been constructed in the center of the city. Alongside these were a number of dilapidated houses. When I asked what the perspective was on this, he informed me that the priority was not on stores and office buildings but for working class homes in areas other than the center of the cities. My mind then went back to the United States where, in almost all metropolitan areas, there has been tremendous construction of office buildings and middle and upper-class housing, with little allocated for working people, the poor Black population in particular.

As for vacations in holiday resorts provided by the trade unions and other organizations, the numbers of people provided for increase from year to year. In 1949, 162,000 people visited the Baltic Coast; in 1968, 1,520,000, including 75,000 foreigners. In the same year, 2 million children went to holiday camps.

Or, let us examine the concern of a Socialist government for old people. Old age pensions increased several times since 1950. The minimum pension in 1950 was 65 marks; today, it is 150. These increases must be seen against the decline in prices. A contrary situation exists in the U.S.A., where people on old age assistance find it exceedingly difficult to keep up with the rising cost of living, etc. Medical services in the G.D.R. likewise increased. The following chart illustrates these changes:

	1949	1967
Hospital beds per 10,000 inhabitants	98	114
Polyclinics	180	436
Outpatient centers	520	810
rural outpatient centers	88	368
Sanitary stations headed by doctors and nurses	2,067	3,331
Community stations headed by nurses	2,400	4,758
Cure facilities	–	182
Beds in cure facilities	–	36,910

Rationalization in industry and a new technology is accompanied by an improvement in conditions, so the workers join enthusiastically in increasing productivity. Consequently, the G.D.R. is already planning for the rest of this century. These plans include the greatest possible development of science and industry. They include training the young generation, the citizens of tomorrow, to use effectively the benefits of science.

In order to see how this is taking place, I visited a general polytechnical school in the County of Karl Marx Stadt, one of the largest industrial areas.

Before going to the school I met and spoke with the workers in a textile machinery plant. It produces machinery for the textile mills. The workers escorted me through the plant and showed me the whole production process. What struck me most was the enthusiasm they showed when they described the new machines which increased their productivity. Such a situation would be most difficult to find in my country where the introduction of new technology makes workers fear losing their jobs.

I saw another example of why they can be so enthusiastic when I visited a workers' rest home in a mining town which is run by the miners' trade union.

I have never had the opportunity to go to Miami Beach in the U.S. and check out the places where only the rich can relax. But thinking of what I have seen in movies or heard described, I feel safe in saying that this rest home has all the conveniences of such places, and in some respect, as far as women and children are concerned, more so.

The profits of the big corporations go into the hands of a few, the rich. So only they can afford to live in such luxury. But here in this land of Socialism part of the income from the workers' production is used to provide facilities such as I had the pleasure to see. These facilities are available for all workers and their families to enjoy.

From the plant and the rest home I went to a polytechnical center in the town of Aue. This, too, is in a mining town. Polytechnical training is part of the curriculum of all schools in the county. In most cases training is carried out direct in the factories. But due to the situation in mining, this particular center is located outside the factory in the town.

Here I saw in life how the G.D.R. is training its

future citizens, the children, to use the new technology. Moreover, I saw in practice how the distinction between manual and mental labor is being overcome.

All children between the ages of eleven and sixteen, from all schools of the town, are required to spend one day a week at this training center. It matters not whether a student eventually will become a professional or mental worker or a laborer, all are required to learn some basic skills at the machines and in manual labor.

The curriculum at the center requires:

    3 hours productive work

    2 hours theory and technical drawing

    2 hours experiments in physics and chemistry.

In polytechnical centers such as this, the entire new generation in the G.D.R. are being trained to use further advances in science and technology.

Coming as I do from a society in which manual labor is viewed by most with contempt, where such labor is boring and is done merely for material considerations, I saw the man and woman of the future in the making, people whose whole being is devoted to the development of their creative and productive talents, including manual skills. I saw a people in the making where intellectual snobbishness, arrogance and conceit is becoming a thing of the past. For in the new society a doctor, a man or woman of science, a writer or an artist will also have some concrete skills of use in production, and can therefore identify him- or herself with the working class in a more meaningful manner.

These developments are of great importance for my people, the Afro-Americans, who for more than three centuries have been the "hewers of wood and drawers of water" in American society. All the dirtiest and hardest work is consigned to people with a black skin.

It is clear that given the same circumstances as I found here we will learn to see labor as an honorable affair, a necessity of life and a possibility for creative work. Moreover, manual labor will be seen as a matter of keeping good health.

The whole of society in one form or another will know the meaning of labor by hand as well as by brain.

Thus the children of the G.D.R., like the children of other Socialist communities, are pioneers for the man and woman of the future.

CHAPTER 6

The G.D.R. and the Socialist Community

It has become fashionable these days in Western capitalist nations to laud the achievements of the German Democratic Republic. There is even talk in some higher circles of facing up to realities and recognizing the G.D.R. on a diplomatic level. Of late, there have appeared a number of books in English which make these points.

The authors of several such books discuss the achievements of the G.D.R., consciously or unconsciously leaving out the socialist background both in the G.D.R. and in the world socialist system to which it belongs. Some say that they are mainly due to the industrious character and superb organizational qualities which are traditional of Germans. There are also those who, while hailing the achievements, claim that they have been made in spite of the close relations of the G.D.R. to the Soviet Union and the Socialist community.

These arguments are not well founded. They are a by-product of the refusal to face up to realities. No doubt, the G.D.R. had a background and tradition of a people highly trained in science and with a sense of discipline and organization, characteristics which made Germans famous. These attributes can be used for or against progress. In Hitler's time they were misused to build up one of the most efficient armies that ever set foot on a battlefield for purposes of conquest and oppression. In our times, since the emergence of the G.D.R., these qualities have been used to improve conditions of the German people, to promote friendship and peace, and to build a better world.

But these qualities do not suffice to explain the rise of the German Democratic Republic to a position of world eminence. The main reason for these achievements was the establishment of a nationally owned sector of the economy and, later, a Socialist system, as described in preceding chapters. Socialism meant planning the economy and making rational use of it so that priorities could be set which would give the best possible results for further development.

As the history of the last twenty years shows, the role of the Soviet Union, its cooperative relations with the G.D.R. and the other socialist states, was of prime importance.

An outstanding example of the aid given by the Soviet Union to the G.D.R. was in the chemical industry. With the cooperation of Czechoslovakia, Poland and Hungary, a "Friendship Pipeline" was constructed in 1963 which brought oil into the country. It is over 3,000 miles long. In 1967 alone, over 4 million tons of oil flowed through this line and were processed in the G.D.R. This accelerated the growth of the chemical industry since, from one million tons of oil, chemical products can be produced which would require about 8 million tons of lignite coal.

Thus the Friendship pipeline became an invaluable aid in building the economy of the G.D.R. Today the chemical industry per capita is second only to the United States. In 1967 approximately 13 percent of the industrial production was based on the chemical industry.

An examination of the growth of every industry will show that the results achieved could not have been attained without the fullest cooperation of the Soviet Union and the Socialist community. Elsewhere, the division of labor between nations is a one-sided affair: it benefits, almost without exception, the more powerful nations. Not so here: The existence of a community of Socialist nations and the new forms of cooperation embodied in the Council of Mutual Economic Aid (CMEA) brought into existence a new type of relationship among nations based on the full equality of the partners and the principle of mutual benefit. The aim is to strengthen each of the Socialist states in the community. On this point, the statement of the Central Committee of the Communist Party of the Soviet Union to the XXIV Congress declares:

> "Should one fail to rely on the general laws and allow for the concrete historic characteristics of each country, it would be impossible to build Socialism. Without taking into account these two factors, it is also impossible to develop correct relations between the Socialist states."
> (L. I. Brezhnev, "Statement of Account of the CC of the CPSU," Moscow/Berlin, 1971, p. 10.)

These are the guide lines for the CMEA. It has brought great benefits to all socialist countries.

Jointly, these countries have tackled successfully

many fundamental economic questions as, for instance, the supply of raw materials, the establishment of new industrial units, the development of transport, the mutual supply of essential means of production and of consumer goods. Especially owing to extensive deliveries by the U.S.S.R., the CMEA countries are almost able to be independent of non-socialist countries in important raw materials and combustibles, e.g. hard coal (98 percent), oil (96 percent), and iron ore (about 80 percent). The Friendship Pipeline at present transports annually 33 million tons of Soviet oil into Hungary, Poland, Czechoslovakia and the G.D.R. and has provided the raw materials to develop the petrochemical industries of these countries, resulting in expanding the production of plastics, synthetic fibers, fertilizers and many other products. The oil deliveries of the Soviet Union to the fraternal countries, amounting to 138 million tons in the 1966–70 period, will attain the level of 243 million tons in the 1970–75 period. To this end, the pipeline capacity will be further extended. Another increase in Soviet deliveries of natural gas is intended.

The railroad transportation system established by the CMEA has been beneficial to all the countries concerned. The cars brought in remain the property of the country concerned. Their common usage, however, yields substantial advantages for each country, such as acceleration of the movement of trains and transportation of goods, fewer empty runs, and technological progress (the use now of only standardized cars).

The foregoing should suffice to show the outstanding role played by the Soviet Union and other socialist countries in the economic development of the G.D.R.

Postwar developments in that part of Germany occupied by the Western powers were utterly different. U.S. imperialism, in the pursuit of its announced goal that the next half of the twentieth century would be the "American Century," like an octopus in the postwar world, reached out to take over ownership of many industries in other countries. Today, the U.S.S.R. does not own or control a single industry in the German Democratic Republic. But, can it be seriously argued that the same situation exists in West Germany, the Federal German Republic, in its relations to the U.S.A.?

"U.S. firms now control more than 40 percent of the total car production and more than 50 percent of the capacity of oil refineries. Furthermore, 15 to 20 percent of all joint stock companies are completely under their control. Approximately 2,000 U.S. firms have established themselves in West Germany, and 1,200 West German firms have become U.S.-controlled." (From DWI Berichte No. 12/70, p. 10 f., published by Deutsches Wirtschaftsinstitut, Berlin–German Economic Institute.) That was the state of affairs in 1970.

Those who speak from lofty heights about "Soviet imperialism" should be advised to check on private U.S. investments abroad, for these reveal the unprecedented extent of control of the world economy by U.S. imperialism. According to data of the U.S.

Department of Commerce, each year since 1950 has witnessed a progressively stepped-up rate of investments in other lands. They reveal the following:

Private Direct Investments of the U.S.A. Abroad
(in million dollars)

	1950	1957	1966	1967	1968
Total	11,788	25,394	54,711	59,542	64,756
Western Europe	1,733	4,151	16,209	17,926	19,386
EEC*	637	1,680	7,584	8,444	8,992
West Germany	204	581	3,077	3,486	3,774
France	217	464	1,758	1,904	1,910
Italy	63	252	1,148	1,246	1,272
Holland	84	191	859	942	1,073
Belgium & Luxembourg	69	192	742	864	963
Great Britain	847	1,947	5,657	6,113	6,703
Switzerland	25	69	1,211	1,322	1,436
Canada	3,579	8,769	16,999	18,097	19,488

("Survey of Current Business," U.S. Dept. of Commerce, Washington, D. C. August 1960 to 1964, September 1965 to 1967, October 1968 and 1969. Not all countries are included, therefore data given for each country do not add up to the column totals.)

* European Economic Community

CHAPTER 7

Democracy at Work

The economic achievements of the German Democratic Republic are widely accepted, but its democratic achievements are much distorted. Most commentators in the Western countries still call the Federal Republic democratic and the G.D.R. totalitarian. These views are in keeping with the hypocritical character of Western capitalist ideology.

Under the banner of "democracy," the Western capitalist powers have waged some of the most predatory wars in history. "Save the world for democracy" was the main slogan of the Allied Powers in World War I. Behind the façade of democracy, racism was permitted to permeate society, while today all that is rotten and degrading in the capitalist world is being defended on the grounds that it would be "undemocratic" to limit the power of millionaires, industrialists and bankers.

With this background, it is understandable that many Western writers deny the existence of democracy in the G.D.R. But the facts are that, together with its economic achievements, it has built one of the most democratic societies in the world. It is a democracy based on new concepts and values, on the elevation of everything that is in the interest of the majority of the people, of the common man. It does not hypocritically pose as being all-inclusive. It has its restrictions, and it is these that the capitalists regard as dictatorial.

The democratic structure of the G.D.R. ties in with some of the thoughts expressed by the great dramatist, Bertolt Brecht, who, some twenty years ago, urged the Federal Republic to do what had been done in the G.D.R. He called for

1. Full freedom for books, with one restriction;
2. Full freedom for the theatre, with one restriction;
3. Full freedom for the visual arts, with one restriction;
4. Full freedom for music, with one restriction;
5. Full freedom for films, with one restriction.

The restriction: No freedom for books or works of art which glorify war or represent it as inevitable or which encourage racial hatred.

If there is one thing that characterizes the emergence of the socialist system in the G.D.R., it is that each step toward socialism has had the consent of the people.

Western imperialists portray the socialist system as an upheaval in which a minority forces its will upon the majority. Thus, socialist revolutions are characterized as not expressing the will of the great majority of the people.

Nothing can be further from the truth. Any serious examination of socialist revolutions beginning with the Russian Revolution of 1917, will show the contrary. Especially is this true of the process which brought socialism to the G.D.R.

It is possible, under certain circumstances, for parties advocating socialism to win power either through parliamentary means or by extra-parliamentary methods. However, in most cases, large masses have not yet been won for socialism. They rally around parties of socialism because they stand for certain demands unobtainable through other parties. Therefore they give the Communists and other socialist-oriented forces a mandate to take power. Such was the case in the eastern part of Germany. The majority were not yet united for socialist purposes, but they were for anti-fascist, peaceful ones.

The Socialist Unity Party recognized this fact and did not try to force socialism upon the people. From the very beginning, a structure was established which allowed for varying ideologies so long as they were anti-fascist. This continued through the years and today, twenty-six years later, the Socialist (Communist) sector is dominant in the new society. This has come about with the consent of the people. However, even today, there is still a small minority who do not accept socialism; but they, too, have a voice and a vote.

Statistics from the *Yearbook for 1970* show: Socialist (government-owned) factories, 3,193; privately owned, 3,416; and those of an intermediate status (state participation with individuals in the form of cooperatives, etc.) 5,646.

Some wrong conclusions may be drawn from these figures because, if you were to add the number of privately owned factories to the semi-private, they would constitute a majority. So the figures by themselves do not tell the whole story. Most of the private enterprises are small businesses, such as repair and services and those distributing commodities.

A more correct appraisal of the socialization of the economy can be obtained from data indicating number of workers employed: In state-owned factories, 2,379,000; in those with state-participation, 359,000; and those privately owned, 79,000. These figures show that the basic form of the economy is Socialist. Nevertheless, those who operate in the private sector of the economy are provided with the means to continue, while efforts are made to convince them to come over to socialism. These take various forms:

1. Craftsmen's Production Cooperatives.
2. Commission Traders (retailers selling goods supplied by the state trading organization on commission).
3. Partnership of the state in private factories.

At present, there are 7,250 enterprises with state partnership; 4,351 Craftsmen's Production Cooperatives; 3,638 private enterprises, mainly in light industry; 127,454 private craftsmen, and 22,848 commission traders.

Farm cooperatives were first formed in 1952 and, by 1960, the socialization of agriculture was completed.

During and after the transition to socialism, the G.D.R. maintained its political structure which included parties representing middle class strata and non-Marxist, especially Christian parts of the population. The leading party is the Socialist Unity Party (SED), founded in 1946, when the Communist Party and the Social-Democratic Party united. It represents the working class.

Other parties are the Christian Democratic Union (CDU). Its members are of Protestant or Catholic faith and include priests and functionaries of various churches. The CDU believes that Socialism implements the basic demands for peace on earth and true charity. Its members fulfill the humanist obligations of Christians by supporting the socialist society and co-operating with the Marxists.

Then there is the Liberal Democratic Party (LDPD). The LDPD carries on the revolutionary and democratic traditions of the German bourgeoisie and helps to implement their aims and humanist ideals on the basis of socialism. It works for the active participation of the middle class and of small and medium businessmen in socialist construction.

The Democratic Peasants' Party (DBD) is the first genuinely democratic farmers' party in German history. It unites cooperative farmers and professionals and trades associated with farm production. The DBD follows the revolutionary traditions of the German peasants against feudal and capitalist oppression. Today, this party strives to develop a modern socialist agriculture. Some 3,000 of its members are chairmen of agriculture production cooperatives, and 12,000 are on executive boards.

The National Democratic Party of Germany (NDPD) was founded in 1948. It exerts a great influence on its members in persuading them to work actively for peace, democracy and socialism.

All these parties, together with other organizations

of the people, constitute what is called the National Democratic Front, and it is through a process of refinement within this Front that all important decisions are made.

All parties are represented in the People's Chamber, the G.D.R.'s governing body. The leading role and great authority of the Socialist Unity Party is universally recognized, but this does not mean that the other parties have no influence. An example of the participation of these parties in economic planning is the fact that they contributed 240 pages of proposals to the Draft Directive for the Five Year Plan for 1971-75.

Each party has its basic organizations and resources, enabling it to participate in national affairs. It has its own structure, based on members' groups. Each one has a central newspaper and county papers. Aside from the SED newspapers, their total daily circulation is 732,000. In addition, each party publishes journals or bulletins for its officials. Each has its own publishing house. In 1970, the LDPD published 22 titles–192,400 books; the NDPD issued 53 titles–877,000 books, and the CDU, 46 titles–419,000 books. Each party has a large central school. Thus, each party can participate according to its strength.

In discussions with people in the National Democratic Front, I was told that things did not always run smoothly, that there were differences on practical issues, but that, gradually, their ability to cooperate and work toward socialism was improving. In the course of change, some people embraced Socialism but

119

still retained ideas and habits differing from those of the leading party of Socialism, the SED.

This represents a multi-party system which is giving everyone a chance of taking part in political life and building socialism within the frame he chooses.

But, if I was impressed with these developments in interparty relations, I was even more struck by the participation of the people in government. It is here that many seek for answers as to how people on lower levels can participate in government affairs. What possibility has the individual to exert his influence? In the G.D.R. no major decision is made on any level without consulting those concerned.

How laws are made here should be studied by those who wish to improve the democratic processes in the so-called democracies. There, laws emanate from political parties or governmental officials and then are debated in Congress or Parliament. Occasionally, hearings are held, where people's organizations may participate. But this is rare and limited.

This is not the case in the G.D.R. No matter the source of a proposal, it goes through a process of discussion among the people before it is passed. For example, the new Constitution in 1968 went through the following process: 11 million citizens discussed the draft in about 750,000 meetings. A total of 12,454 proposals were submitted, and the Constitution Commission made 118 changes on the basis of these proposals. On April 6, 11,975,889 citizens took part in a plebiscite on the draft, with 11,536,803 approving it, or 94.49 percent of those entitled to vote. For the first time in German history, the people had given themselves a Constitution. Three days later, Walter Ulbricht, Chairman of the Council of State signed it.

What was true in the case of the Constitution applies to all basic laws.

In discussion of the Labor Code in 1961, 325,000 meetings were held with 7 million participating. A million persons spoke in the discussion and 23,000 suggestions for changes were submitted. Five hundred suggestions for improving the Draft Youth Law were made before its adoption in 1964. Two million participated in the discussion of the Education Law in 1965. That year, 750,000 persons were heard on the Family Code, making 23,737 suggestions, resulting in 230 alterations. Fifty thousand discussed the Penal Code in 1967–68, and 8,141 proposals for changes were made.

Some say that the unions in the G.D.R. are not free to strike for better conditions. Let us examine this, as I did on one of my visits.

Democracy is also practiced in the factories. It begins there! There is where material values are produced and where technological revolution produces many new problems. In the long run efficiency and living standards are determined there.

For example, since the inception of the New Economic System, year-end bonuses can be paid in state enterprises. In the Brandenburg worsted spinning mill, the workers had received year-end bonuses of only 20 and 50 marks for 1967. This was unfair, especially as the managers got 1,000 marks and more. The employees, mostly women, appealed to the regional trade union committee and, shortly thereafter, the shop stewards met. They were assured that the district secretaries of the SED, trade union officials and staff members of the Association of Nationally Owned Textile Enterprises, to which the mill is affiliated, would examine the matter. The investigation revealed that the managers had acted incorrectly and selfishly. The bonus fund for 1967 was slim, since the mill had not earned any surplus due to faulty management, and the fund was insufficient to pay a year-end bonus at the legal amount of one-third of the monthly wage. In such cases, no bonuses are provided for, and, if this procedure had been followed, the managers would not have received bonuses, either. But they had acted otherwise.

However, their plan failed. The workers' party, the unions and state organs found that the management had violated a vital principle of Socialist democracy by not informing the workers of the mill's situation and failing to seek ways of restoring profitability by discussions with the workers. The economic, technical and production managers, as well as the head accountant, were fired. The women workers themselves decided to pay more attention in the future to the problems of the enterprise. One of them, Margarete Fischer, said: "This solution proves again that we have an essential voice as socialist owners."

I was interested in the extent of women's participation in the new society, so I interviewed a number of people, including Ilse Thiele, President of the Women's Democratic League. I was deeply impressed by what she said—that the whole of society was geared to creating the kind of conditions necessary for the fullest participation of women in its affairs. This does not, of course, mean that problems do not exist. There are still those of ideology and remnants of the old system still prevail. However, the important thing is that the direction has been set and the achievements are such that one can be confident that the day is near when women will no longer be subordinated to men but will increasingly participate in the nation's affairs, with time to rear their children and still have leisure for cultural and social pursuits.

To facilitate the employment of more women, additional crèches, nursery schools, kindergartens and after-school day-care centers will be available in 1975, as provided in the Five Year Plan. For every 1,000 children, there will be 290–300 places in crèches; 750 in nursery schools and kindergartens, and 660 in day-care centers.

In the U.S., the government sponsors programs only for children to age six. There are some nursery schools, but these are private and many working class families cannot afford them.

In the People's Chamber in the G.D.R., women make up 30.6 percent of the Deputies; in the West German Parliament, they constitute 6.6 percent (34 out of 518). In the G.D.R., women are in leading governmental positions: 5 are members of the State Council; one is a Minister; 3 are Deputy Ministers; 11 are Chairmen of County Councils; 4 are Lord Mayors, and 1,593 others are Mayors. In West Germany, one woman is a Minister, one a State Secretary; 2 are Parliamentary State-Secretaries, and one is a Vice-President of Parliament.

With respect to religious views, the Constitution

provides for religious freedom. There are about 8,000 parishes in the eight Evangelical bishoprics, with 5,500 pastors, 5,500 catechists (teachers of religion employed by the church); 6,100 deacons, and 4,000 parish helpers, plus other church employees.

The Catholic Church is in a minority, except in three smaller districts. It has 1,500 priests and other members of Catholic Orders; 2,700 nuns, teachers and church employees.

There are 27 free church and smaller religious communities, with 700 pastors, deacons, etc. In addition to Sundays, legal holidays include two days at Christmas, Good Friday, and Whit Monday.

No differences exist in treatment of the various confessions. Protestants, Catholics, free churches (League of Evangelical Free Church Communities), Methodists, New Apostolic Church, Jews and smaller religious groups have equal rights.

Catholics in the G.D.R. realize ever more clearly that there is no discrepancy between the will to peace expressed by Pope John XXIII and Pope Paul VI, and the peace efforts of the G.D.R. Thousands of copies of "Pacem In Terris" were distributed to Catholics. On his pilgrimage to Palestine, Pope Paul sent a message to the Chairman of the G.D.R. State Council.

Six universities, at Berlin, Leipzig, Halle, Jena, Rostock and Greifswald, have theological faculties to train Protestant clergy. The students receive state stipends on the same basis as do other students. The state allocates 38,000 Marks for each theology student, and 4.2 million marks a year for lectures, research, travel, etc.

The churches, especially the Protestant, have many training institutions: 132 seminaries and colleges, residential schools, music schools, nurses' training schools and schools for deacons and parish helpers.

The rights of Christians are guaranteed by the Constitution. Articles 41 and 48 deal with religion and religious communities in the G.D.R. These communities are represented in the People's Chamber through the Christian-Democratic Union, as well as having members in most of the Ministries. I participated in a public session on the program for human rights on a platform with the Chief Justice of the highest court in the land who is one of the leaders of the Christian-Democratic Union.

The participation of youth in the management of the state is another milestone in the extension of democracy. Since its founding, the workers' and farmers' state has paid special attention to youth. In 1950, the People's Chamber, the Parliament of the G.D.R., passed the "Law on Participation of Youth in the Construction of the German Democratic Republic and the Promotion of Youth Activity in Schools and Vocations, Sports and Recreation." The law ensures all young people the right to political co-determination, to work and recreation, to education, etc. Possibilities open up to the young generation it never had before.

As a result of this approach, the Free German Youth has its own Deputies, numbering 40, in the Chamber, with an average age of 24.7 years. Youth participate in all activities.

I also wanted to see to what extent people on the community level participate in the affairs of government. I was motivated by the fact that Blacks in the U.S.A. have for years been struggling to take part in the affairs of their communities. They seek some measure of control, not only in formulating the laws, but also in their execution. As of now, they have few opportunities to do so. I wanted to know what the situation was in a socialist society.

In the G.D.R., there is an organ of government that does not exist in cities of the U.S. at the community level. Government in our cities is determined by individuals elected from precincts or assembly districts, but there are no governing bodies at the community level.

Just the opposite is true in the G.D.R. There are Community Councils, elected by the people in the community, often with jurisdiction in determining governmental processes as they affect local affairs. But participation in their own affairs is also facilitated by organizations not run by professional politicians.

Some 207,000 citizens out of a population of 17 million, are active as elected Deputies. Five hundred of them are members of the supreme body, the People's Chamber; the others in County and District Councils, municipal assemblies, municipal borough bodies, etc. In addition to the Deputies, there are 400,000 other citizens without a Deputy's mandate, who directly cooperate with the elected Deputies in the "standing commissions" and various *ad hoc* bodies. The former also play a decisive role in dealing with social tasks of many kinds.

Three hundred thousand citizens—members of political parties and non-party people—work in the local

National Front Committees. They are active largely in residential areas and through public meetings and discussions organized by tenants' associations to see that all political and personal questions are answered or solved. They work to improve the functioning of trade organizations and services. They check on social and medical assistance to the sick and aged. They help ensure a just distribution of housing, concern themselves with traffic safety, and work to beautify their surroundings.

Also, the administration of justice is in the hands of the people. In the G.D.R., judges are elected, and most of them are daughters and sons of workers and farmers. Smaller offenses are no longer dealt with by the courts, but by lay "dispute commissions" with a total of 189,767 members. (Every larger nationally owned enterprise has such a body.) 55,000 citizens work in arbitration commissions, situated mostly in residential areas, cooperatives and private undertakings; and 48,000 are lay judges with the same rights as judges in court. These figures show that every fortieth citizen has an honorary office in the administration of justice, and that upholding the law is becoming the concern of all working people.

Many transgressions against discipline, petty theft, minor civil law disputes, private quarrels and insults, are settled by the people themselves. In 1967, in more than 80 percent of civil disputes, amicable settlement was reached or the matter clarified without going to court. Here is manifest the gradual transfer of governmental tasks directly into the hands of social bodies, such as the "dispute commissions" in production centers, which are elected bodies supported by the trade unions, to administer justice.

Thus, when one totals up these aspects of democracy at work in the G.D.R. and contrasts it with what takes place in the so-called democracies, one can see that it is only when the working class holds power that all strata of the people can truly participate in the democratic processes.

CHAPTER 8

Education Geared to Developing a New Man

The highest achievement of the German Democratic Republic has been the transformation of the people. Their educational system has been largely responsible for this achievement.

What was the basis of this success? What was the process that they had to go through? What was the content of those processes, as well as the forms?

Educational work was as difficult as that in the field of economics. Intellectual poverty was an evil inherited from the old order.

There were many children between 13 and 18 who in 1945 had not had regular schooling for some years. There were then in the East zone 4,114 one-room schools. There was great scarcity of everything and many youngsters had turned to black marketeering to live. A quarter of the schools were unusable and in the towns up to 85 percent were destroyed.

Teachers were infected by Nazi doctrines, and had to be rigorously removed.

After cleaning the staff of Nazis and working out new curricula, new priorities were established. This was the 1946 reform. It put foremost the education of workers' children.

As I studied what measures were undertaken, the thought occurred to me that this is precisely what Black people in the United States are calling for today, namely special measures to undo the harm that had been done to these youth—to give them priorities that have existed mainly for children of the middle and upper classes—categories where Black people are very few. This is especially true at the university level. Many working class youth dropped out of high school before graduating, or had been given inferior training while at the high school level; and to meet the problem, special measures are required in instruction as well as in conditions. The educational reforms in the G.D.R. provide an experience that could be useful in the United States.

The G.D.R. set up Workers' and Peasants' Faculties, to prepare such children for university. They were attached to the universities with the task of preparing students quickly for the university. This meant a new content based on their experience, new teaching methods and a dedicated teaching staff.

Many white, middle class teachers in our Black ghettoes have this difficulty. They find it difficult to convey their ideas in terms of the life style of the students making it easier to grasp.

These problems had to be met in the G.D.R. and a new staff trained. Priorities for workers meant that temporarily some children from other strata had to wait.

I met a young lady with a middle class background who had to wait to enter the university. She said it was really hard but in time she understood it and accepted it. Today, she is a doctoral candidate. Her education was merely delayed. This is true of thousands now in high positions.

Education starts at age three, with kindergarten. Already at this pre-school age, children learn to co-operate and become social beings. They have constant medical care from nurses at government expense.

The next level is the ten-year polytechnical secondary school with three stages: grades 1 to 3; 4 to 6 and 7 to 10. This training is of great importance. Children receive general instruction and technical and practical skills, in wood, metal and plastics. In schoolgardens, they learn horticulture. Technical training continues throughout secondary schools, so all children are educated to live in modern society. I found much stress on this, as the G.D.R. is planning ahead to the year 2000, where the new technology will become increasingly important.

Universities and colleges have reached a high level. Their number rose from 6 universities in 1945 to 44 universities and colleges in 1968. The universities of Berlin, Leipzig, Halle, Jena, Rostock, the Technical University of Dresden and the Mining Academy in Freiberg have a long tradition.

In 1968, a total of 110,200 students were enrolled at these institutions. In addition, there were many young people from 60 other countries studying under the same conditions as their German fellows.

Here are also 189 vocational colleges: engineering-technological, economic, medical, pedagogic and artistic fields are the main ones. In 1968, they had 140,590 students.

Graduates of twelve-year secondary-school may go to university or college, whereas the leaving certificate of the ten-class secondary school qualifies for admission to a vocational college. Studies are free for all citizens. Eighty percent of university and college students and 92 percent of those in vocational colleges receive grants that are sufficient to cover everyday needs.

Gifted and socially active students may get the Pieck Scholarship of 300 marks monthly or the Marx Scholarship (450).

The course at universities and colleges lasts four or five years (except in medicine and chemistry), and at vocational colleges three. After a broad training in basic subjects, there is increasing specialization. Much emphasis is put on bringing students into contact with the practical side of their future sphere of work at an early stage. As a result the students not only as a rule do well at public examinations, but find it easier to master the problems of their profession.

There is close collaboration between teachers and parents. In countries where children are taught one thing in school and parents at home teach them something else, it is difficult to avoid serious conflicts and psychological problems. But where the parents are directly drawn into the teaching processes, where the teacher and the parent are united in educational matters, the chances for educational successes are infinitely greater.

School problems are taken up in parents' advisory councils, which meet regularly with teachers every six to eight weeks. The councils make suggestions on how the teachers can best win children's confidence and attain higher results in learning. This is important because the teacher especially the young teacher may come from a different environment than that of the community and may not be able to reach the high level demanded by educational authorities without the parents' aid.

Such is the background of the new education in the G.D.R. As a result, the achievements here as in economic areas, have broken through the blockade of lies about the "land beyond the wall."

People who visit the G.D.R. and study the system often leave impressed. Helmut Lindemann, a journalist from Munich in West Germany wrote:

> ". . . The positive impression of such a trip simply cannot be duplicated in the Federal Republic.
> "One feels, from a survey of kindergarten to university, that the G.D.R. is a great deal ahead of us educationally, because there they have a definite plan under which they can work for decades, even if the necessity for correction emerges, which will surely be the case."
> (Helmut Lindemann, "The Red Educational Paradise," *Abendzeitung*, Munich, July 23, 1965.)

Joachim Besser, another West German journalist, visited the East and wrote:

> ". . . The G.D.R. has 44 universities and colleges, with 100,000 students. Their social origin was in 1965: workers, 31.8 percent; employees, 26 percent; members of agricultural cooperatives, 5.6 percent; professions 28.9 percent, independent tradesmen, 5.1 percent . . . The greatest advance

is the fact that the workers make up almost a third of the students, compared with 5 percent here."

(Joachim Besser, "The G.D.R. Seen Objectively," *Kölner Stadt-Anzeiger*, Cologne, December 7, 1966.)

Recognition of developments is also to be observed in the U.S. Recently, there have appeared a number of books referring to achievements in the G.D.R. I was impressed by John Dornberg:

"East Germany is attuned to youth, a land where suffrage begins at 18, some plant managers are in their 20's and the heads of industrial trusts, in their 30's. East Germany's young are impatient for power.

"Young East Germans are the product of the G.D.R.'s *most* revolutionary development: an educational system that has resulted in equality of opportunity unparalleled in German history. In twenty years the regime has successfully cleansed the school system of all the cobwebs of retardation, authoritarianism, reaction and class distinction. It is rare for any institution in the G.D.R. to elicit even grudging acknowledgment from West Germany, but its schools have won almost unqualified admiration. Economically, East Germany remains a decade behind the Federal Republic. Pedagogically, it is several decades ahead."

(John Dornberg, *The Other Germany*, Doubleday, Garden City, New York 1968, p. 307.)

Dornberg makes a comparison between the two German states:

"Both Germanys entered the postwar period with the same system of education. West Germany's remained essentially unchanged. What transpired in the G.D.R., however, is nothing less than a pedagogic explosion, which once prompted Hamburg's influential weekly *Die Zeit* to comment that 'it is inconceivable that the two school systems ever had a common origin.'

"Whereas only 30 percent of West German youths receive ten or more years of schooling, in the G.D.R. this group represents more than 70 percent. Only 4.3 percent of West German youths go on to college. In the G.D.R. it is already 15 percent and Ulbricht has promised that it will be 25 percent by 1970 . . . The number of East German universities and colleges has increased from six, at the end of the war, to forty-four in 1967 with another 1,000 specialized institutes, including 212 technical schools of higher learning. The total number of university and college students in East Germany in 1967 was 110,000 plus 129,000 in technical schools, compared to a total of 288,000 in West Germany whose populations is 3.5 times larger."
(Ibid. p. 309.)

This author unlike many others, places the social system at the heart of what has transpired.

"At the root of this education explosion is one of

Socialism's oldest maxims: Knowledge is Power. That was the slogan of the nineteenth-century workers' education societies from which both German Socialism and Communism originated. It was a principle to which the SED–an amalgamation, after all, of both Communist and Social Democrats–paid special attention when it set out to reform education in the 1940's and 1950's. That reform had three distinct goals: to raise the general level of education, to eradicate all class and social distinctions and to equip all children with both theoretical and practical knowledge."

(Ibid. p. 310.)

The Eighth Party Congress of the SED envisages the further strengthening of education in the next five years. It may be seen what the future holds for the youth who will guide this country tomorrow. They will, without doubt, represent one of the highest levels of humankind that the world has ever seen.

CHAPTER 9

Education Against Racism

In the course of interviewing government depart-
ments and agencies, I visited the Deputy Minister of
Education and members of his staff. In our conversation, I said that I was deeply impressed with the
children who had rallied to the defense of Angela
Davis. Everywhere I went I found manifestations of
love and concern for her. What struck me most is
what the children are doing. Wherever I had gone,
members of the Free German Youth had asked me to
convey to her their feelings. They showed me postcards they had prepared and sent out, petitions
collected and pictures they had drawn. In several
instances, they had named their summer camps in her
honor. I also learned that immediately after she was
arrested, the children spontaneously collected over a
million signatures which they sent to U.S. authorities.
I asked whether such activities had been organized
or were they actually spontaneous. They replied that
in a certain sense they were spontaneous because no
one had instructed them to do it; but in another sense
they were not spontaneous as these children had been
trained in the schools to react to injustices against
Black people in the United States.

I asked: What kind of education are you conducting that brings out the marvelous qualities dis-
played by these children? They said their curriculum

from the kindergarten to the university, carried messages about Black America.

Present at our discussion was the man who was Head of the Department of Curriculum in the Ministry of Education. He invited me to look at the textbooks used in the schools. These were translated into English and I went through books set up for all levels. Never have I seen the problems of Black America integrated into the general school system as I saw them there. Here is an example that in my country can and must be emulated.

The following represents a few selections from these books. Some are rather lengthy, but I present them because they are so unusual that the world ought to know how the youth in the G.D.R. are being trained against racism.

The following are from *Lesebuch*: *Klasse 2*, Berlin, 1970–Reader for seven-year-olds.

CHILDREN'S DAY

1.
Come, let's hold hands
And celebrate a feast today,
Remembering the other kids
Of all the peoples everywhere.

2.
First of June it is today,
Children's Day for every child
Whether he is yellow or brown,
Or black or white.

3.
Let us dance and skip
Let us all be gay

Let our songs be heard
Also far away.

4.
All the kids on earth
Want to stand side by side
And the banner of peace
Shall protect their lives.

(p. 72.)

LETTERS TRAVEL ROUND THE WORLD

Letters travel round the world
Like the wind and the clouds,
Frontiers may not hinder them
Flying round to all the children
Who are on friendly terms.
Over mountains, over oceans
We send love to all our friends
and our friendly call
Will be answered by them all.
And afterwards we'll meet again,
Merrily we'll meet again.

YOUNG PIONEERS' MARCH

We know: in all the countries
Throughout the whole wide world
Young Pioneers like you and me
Are ready to be our friends.

Jack is an American Negro boy. He lives with his parents and five brothers and sisters in a miserable hut in the suburb of a big city. Jack's father is a mechanic in a car factory. Since he is a Negro, he gets less pay than white workmates. And often he is unemployed.

Jack will often remember the day we refer to here.

It was early September. As in other American cities, the school year is beginning. Hundreds of children are on their way to school. There are only nine Negroes and Jack is one of them. These nine are the first Negroes allowed to go to this school, which until then was open only to white children.

From afar, the children recognize the big school building. But what are all the people at the entrance waiting for?

When Jack and the other Black children want to enter the school, they are received by a yelling and hissing crowd: "What do you want here? This school is for whites only." But Jack's parents have told him that Negroes should have the same rights as the others. Without paying attention to the threats, he and his friends enter. A white, wealthy farmer tries to stop them. He has a stick in his hand and wants to hit Jack. The boy has a close view of his hate-filled face and tries to escape. But the farmer catches him. Furiously he starts beating the defenseless boy. Jack faints and hears as from far off: "Lousy pack of Negroes! We'll show you who is boss here!"

An old white woman takes care of the boy, who is blood-covered. Courageously she shouts to the crowd which is still yelling and preventing the children from entering: "Leave the kids in peace! What have they done to you?"

Then, with her last strength, she carried the boy away.

This is what happened to Jack the first day of school. Only when he reached home did he come to. When he heard his mother's voice he felt safe again. In the evening, his father cheered him up. Jack knows now that what happened this day can happen again. But he also knows:

The Negroes in his country fight for their rights and freedom. Many people in the whole world support them.

The following selection is from a reader in English: "A Negro Looking For a Job," Volk und Wissen, Volkseigener Verlag Berlin, 1970.

Harry Lardner, a young Negro, entered the office of Mr. Hunt, owner of a big Chicago garage.

Harry: "Good morning, Mr. Hunt."

Mr. Hunt: "Ah, it's you, Lardner. What can I do for you?"

Harry: "I've heard you need some workers, Mr. Hunt. That's why I've come."

Mr. Hunt: "I'm afraid I can't help you, Lardner."

Harry: "When you dismissed me three months ago you said you'd give me the first job to open up."

Mr. Hunt: "That's right. But you're late. Why didn't you come yesterday?"

Harry: "I only learned this morning. Mr. Hunt, can't you help me? I need the job badly. My mother has been ill for weeks. You always said you were pleased with my work. You know I'd do the hardest and dirtiest jobs, Mr. Hunt."

Mr. Hunt: "I'd like to help you, Lardner, but things aren't that easy. I'll see what I can do. Ask again in a month. Good-bye, Lardner."

Harry: "Good-bye, Mr. Hunt."

When Harry left, Miss Hill, the secretary, came in.

Miss Hill: "Excuse me, Mr. Hunt. There's a man looking for a job."

Mr. Hunt:	"A Negro?"
Miss Hill:	"No, a white man."
Mr. Hunt:	"All right. Send him in. I think I've got something for him."

FIGHT FOR YOUR CIVIL RIGHTS!

Frank Brown and George Turner, who worked in a Chicago car plant, were on their way home. At a corner a Negro girl handed each of them a leaflet. The men stopped and began to read:

"Our Constitution says that all men are equal, and the President has often said that the 22 million American Negroes have the same rights as whites. But we have not! Our only 'right' is to fight and be killed in dirty wars which are not ours.

"Most of our people are poor. They must live in miserable houses. For one white worker who has no job there are two or three Negroes out of work.

"Our children do not get a good education. The racists do not like our boys and girls in the schools for white children, and they make it difficult for them to go to high school and college.

"In spite of the Civil Rights law they still do not serve us in many restaurants. They may throw us out if we enter their theaters. Your boss says he'll fire you if you vote. The Ku Kluxers threaten to kill you. And the police will only laugh at you if you go to them to complain. They will beat you, shoot you, send you to prison whenever they have a chance.

"But we are not afraid any longer. We know our strength, and we have learned to change things. Help us, black brother! Fight with us for your civil rights, for freedom and equality!

"Join our march on Sunday!

"And you, white brother, march with us! Your enemies are the same as ours!"

"Are you going to join the march?" George asked Frank as they went on. "No," Frank said, "I've got something more interesting to do on Sunday." They passed a restaurant and George invited Frank to have a cup of coffee with him. Suddenly a young Negro came running out of the restaurant, bleeding and screaming. Two white men followed him. George saw what would happen. "Come here," he shouted to the Negro. One of the men tried to attack George. But George was quicker. He gave him a blow that sent him down.

"We'd better get away before they call their companions for help," Frank said.

"Thank you," the Negro said. "They'd have beaten me again if you hadn't helped me."

"Why did they beat you?" Frank asked.

"I don't know. The racists are crazy because there's civil rights march on Sunday."

"Those fascist swine," George said. "I'll join the march. Today it's the Negroes, tomorrow it may be us. What about you, Frank?"

"I think I'd better come along."

The following is from *Education for Today and Tomorrow*, Verlag Zeit im Bild, Dresden, 1970, pp. 21-24.

One of the authors of this pamphlet made a survey and invited 13-year-olds at a secondary school in Berlin-Johannisthal (where he taught) to a discussion on April 13, 1965. The selection of the pupils was accidental (whoever had the time to come), and the theme was not revealed to them until the discussion began. Here are some of the notes, verbatim, shortened only in the case of a few passages that had nothing to do with the subject:

Reischock: "What is actually happening in Georgia, Alabama and other states?"

Peter: "Negroes are fighting for their rights there. They don't have the same rights as whites."

Reischock: "What sort of rights are these?"

Gabi: "For example, voting rights. When there are elections, they are hindered from voting. And very often they don't allow the Negro children into the schools."

Ulli: "The Negroes are fighting against the dis . . . against the dis . . . how do they call it?"

Reischock: "Discrimination."

Ulli: "Yes."

Rainer: "These are also vested rights. In his election speeches President Johnson promised the Negroes equal rights, and now they want to have what has been promised them."

Holger: "It is also there in the American constitution—that everyone should have equal rights. That means also for the Negroes. They organized a Freedom March, where they demonstrated for their rights."

Peter: "The Negroes, as it happens, are more cheaply-paid labor. That is why they oppose equality for Negroes."

Reischock: "Who, then, is fighting here against whom? Is it a struggle of the whites against the Blacks or Blacks against whites?"

Ulli: "No, white people have also fought for the rights of Negroes."

Reischock: "On whose side are you then in this struggle?"

Concentration camp

The German people's inheritance of fascist war: Ruins

The Nuremberg Tribunal

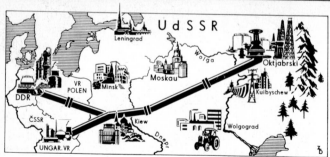

Oil refining station at Schwedt and pipeline from U.S.S.R.:
Symbol of friendship between G.D.R., Poland and Soviet Union

Third World Youth Festival held in Berlin 1951; Berlin will again host the Tenth World Youth Festival in 1973

Children collecting money in the cause of solidarity

A memorable occasion: The visit to G.D.R. of Angela Davis' sister, Fania Jordan

Dr. Ralph Abernathy speaks to students of Humboldt University at demonstration for Angela Davis

Claude Lightfoot at Eighth Party Congress of the Socialist Unity Party of the G.D.R.

A G.D.R. Sing Club with Soviet friends

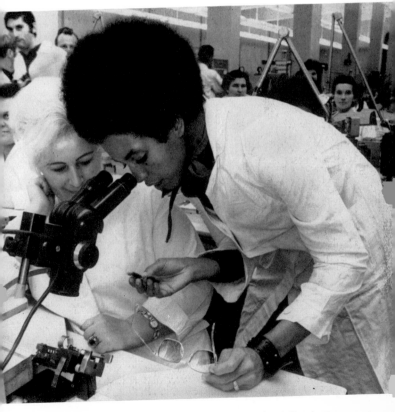

Angela Davis' sister, Fania Jordan, visits the Semi-Conductor plant at Frankfurt on Oder where women of G.D.R. and Poland work together

Help for the valiant
people of Vietnam:
Vietnamese youth
train in the G.D.R.

Young workers of G.D.R. help their Cuban friends harvest
sugar cane

G.D.R. teacher conducting a natural science class in Conakry, Guinea

SS war criminal Hermann Seibold, key figure in the imperialist aggression against the young Republic of Guinea in 1970

"Housing" for foreign workers in West Germany

Racism still lives in the Federal Republic

Young West Germans protest against discrimination in restaurants

West Germans demonstrate for Freedom for Angela Davis

Rainer:	"On the side of the Negroes, naturally. They are people like us and must have the same rights."
Reischock:	"I would like to read you something from a West German newspaper, the *Frankfurter Rundschau*, in which an 18-year-old apprentice said: 'You're naturally more friendly to the white man than to the black.' What do you think of that?"
Sigrid:	"Why does he say that? Perhaps he has never met a Black man."
Hannes:	"I think what he says is nonsense. A friend of ours has a wife who is Indian. She also has a darker skin. If what the apprentice says is true, then our friend should have married a white woman."
Rainer:	"What the apprentice says is pure ignorance. They tell the people that the Blacks threaten the whites. I mean, for example, in the West German newspaper. There, for example, they have also atrocity stories about the Congo."
Bärbel:	"I also think it is nonsense, what the apprentice said. They are all the same people, only they have another skin color. And they have done nothing to us."
Reischock:	"Rainer just mentioned the Congo. Whose side do you take in this conflict?"
Misha:	"We support the Liberation Army, because it fights for liberty in the Congo."
Reischock:	"Are you for or against the Africans?"
Chorus:	"For the Africans!"
Rainer:	"I am also *against* certain Africans. Against Tshombé, for example. He is only a puppet. He is himself against the Africans."

Reischock: "Why are we then—in the Congo, for example—for some Africans and against others?"

Holger: "They are quite different Africans, and what is involved are raw materials, uranium, and the foreign capitalists want to have these."

Hannes: "Some Africans are right and some are not."

Rainer: "At one time Tshombé was the Prime Minister of Katanga and betrayed the Congolese. He is also responsible for the murder of Lumumba."

Ulli: "Tshombé was only bought with gold, and then he did what the imperialists wanted. In Alabama they would probably club him."

(The children now told about the brutalities of the white mercenary troops in the Congo, especially about the one-time first lieutenant of the Nazi army named Müller, with the nickname, Congo Müller. They had seen a television report on the subject.)

Reischock: "Now I would like to read you something else from the same West German newspaper. They asked 13- to 15-year-old children, about your age, which peoples and groups they find sympathetic and which unsympathetic. The result was the following—I shall read it to you: 'Among the clearly sympathetic groups stood the Germans, with 66.1 percent, then the Americans with 50.4 percent, and the Swiss with 35.5. Among the clearly negative and unsympathetic groups, the first was the Russians, with 82.9 percent.' What do you say to that?"

Hannes: "That only shows that they have been taught

	a false attitude. For example, they talk badly about the Russians."
Rainer:	"That is probably also because of fascist teachers, who were against the Russians before and who teach the children the same thing now. That will have the result that they will some day do bad things to other peoples."
Ulli:	"Under the fascists they drilled into the people that all other peoples are our enemies. And that led to all the other things . . ."
Reischock:	"Suppose I now ask you: what peoples do you find sympathetic and which unsympathetic?"
Peter:	"We would find no differences between the peoples. We would only find a difference between oppressed peoples and those who oppress them."
Ulli:	"I like all peoples and am interested in how they are doing–apart from the imperialists, because the imperialists are against their own peoples and against all other peoples. Therefore, I am against them."
Hannes:	"I think that all people are equal. But there are oppressors and those who are oppressed."

(The following is from *Lesebuch Klasse 3*, Berlin 1970–reading book for 8-year-olds, p. 82–84.)

JIMMY AND FRED

The incident narrated below happened in a school in the South of the United States.

When Fred entered the third grade, the teacher seated him beside Jimmy. He was a small Negro boy with white teeth and big clever eyes.

Jimmy smiled at Fred and showed him his treasures: a new pencil and a large red apple. Fred smiles, too.

Jimmy's eyes became still larger. He took the apple in his left hand and placed a finger of his right hand on it. This was to show that he wanted to divide the apple and give Fred half of it.

Fred showed him his new pencil, too, and a big piece of cake, wrapped in paper. He asked Jimmy with his eyes: "Would you like a bit of the cake?"

The Negro boy nodded his head.

During recess, in the yard, Fred did not leave Jimmy's side. They talked to each other:

"What's your name?"

"Fred. And yours?"

"Jimmy."

Without another word, Jimmy gave Fred half of his apple.

"Thanks, Jimmy."

Fred broke his cake into two pieces and said:

"Take it, Jimmy, it tastes good!"

Jimmy did not live far from Fred's home. He waited for him every day and they went to school together. Jimmy did his lessons very well. When Fred did not understand something properly, Jimmy patiently explained it to him.

Fred had other friends in the grade. They liked to be with him because he could invent such nice games; but some did not like it at all that he and Jimmy were close friends.

One afternoon, when Fred and Jimmy entered the

playground, one of his friends said: "Fred, if you bring Jimmy along once again, we won't play with you."

Fred stopped, astonished, took Jimmy's hand and asked:

"Why not?"

"Because my mother has told me not to play with Negro kids," the boy replied.

Jimmy's eyes became very sad. His lips trembled with excitement. He wanted to let Fred's hand go. But Fred seized Jimmy tighter, stepped up to the boy and said angrily: "You can do what your mother says. If you don't want to play with Jimmy, go away. I will do what my mother says. And she says that Negro boys are just as good as all other kids. Jimmy is certainly better and smarter than you are!"

The boy began to stutter: "I, I did not . . ."

"Get going!" Fred interrupted him. "And all the others who don't like Negroes can go, too."

None of the boys budged an inch. They looked at Fred and Jimmy and smiled. The boy who had started the quarrel said once again: "Fred, I didn't mean it, I . . ."

"O.K.," Fred interrupted with satisfaction, "if you want to join our game, you can stay."

Tears of joy glistened in Jimmy's eyes. Fred cried gaily: "Come on, let's play!"

That was not the last time that Fred came to his friend's defense.

One Saturday afternoon, there was an exciting movie at the cinema. Many children went to see it, and Fred and Jimmy, too. They had bought tickets and were just about to enter the auditorium. Fred wanted to sit in the boxes because he could see better there. The woman at the door who took the tickets let him in, but held his

149

friend Jimmy back and said: "You must go upstairs to the balcony."

Fred was surprised and asked: "Why does he have to sit in the balcony? He has the same ticket as I."

The woman shrugged her shoulders and replied: "Negroes are not allowed to sit in the boxes."

"Then we want our money back," Fred said to the woman. "I have come here with my friend, and we want to sit together."

"Drop it, Fred," Jimmy protested. "We have been looking forward so much to the movie! Sit here; I'll go upstairs!"

"No!" Fred cried. "I've come with you, and we'll sit together!"

"But you can see better downstairs," Jimmy remarked.

Fred did not answer. He thought for a minute, then climbed the stairs to the balcony with Jimmy and took a seat with his friend and the other Negro children.

From *Music for the 11th and 12th Grades*, 17- and 18-year-olds, Berlin, 1969, pp. 18–19.

About Jazz

In its different styles, jazz has not only spread over the world, but has also influenced in numerous ways the work of many contemporary composers. Its origin and development are directly connected with the history of the American Negro and its nature can be understood only from the inseparable connection of music and society. "It is an important testimony of the independent culture of the American Negroes, created under American conditions, and expresses by music their social position, feelings and vitality." (André Asriel, G.D.R. composer.)

The history of U.S. Negroes who were deprived of their rights and subject to merciless exploitation, began in the seventeenth century with the slave trade, which led to about 15–20 million Africans being forcibly brought to America. Despite the century-long struggle of progressive white and colored Americans for social equality, Negroes in the United States continue to be deprived of their rights and subjected to racial hatred by the ruling class.

The social and musical foundations of jazz, emerging about 1900, are to be found in this development. Negroes were faced with heavy labor on plantations, to which they were unaccustomed, and this is reflected in their work songs. These had already been sung in Africa, and the peculiarities of their culture were preserved in such songs. White slave owners tolerated, even encouraged such work songs, for they helped to increase productivity.

Typical is the steady change of soloist and choir. While the soloist improvises new texts and lines of melody, the choir replies frequently with an unchanging melody. Sometimes they overlap, which causes a temporary two-voiced polyphony. Occasionally, tools or work movements are used for accompaniment. Since the content largely reflect the feelings of the downtrodden harassed slaves, the songs are not sung "beautifully." Hoarse intonation, overemphasized and vehemently outpressed tones are typical of their music making.

The abolition of slavery (1865) brought certain improvements in living conditions. This made it possible also to use instruments. (Previously, slaves could not use them!) This was an important step in developing instrumental jazz. The first instruments were guitar and banjo. With their help, an individual could make music; transferring the question-answer principle to solo singing and instrumental accompaniment, he could, by improving, become a sort of living newspaper for his Black brothers left in illiteracy.

Thus, the Blues emerged, with a content reflecting the life and thinking of the American Negroes.

Geography for Grade 8 –14-year-olds–Berlin, 1969.

The colonialists attempted to justify this enslavement by the lie that the Africans were, prior to colonialism, socially, economically and culturally still very backward and unable to develop by themselves, without the guidance of Europeans. The facts show the contrary.

An African country, Egypt, was one of the first to produce great economic and scientific achievements. In the rest of North Afria there existed similar developed areas when the peoples of Central and West Europe still lived primitively. In the Sudan, there existed powerful feudal realms which had reached the same level of development as European feudalism of that time. They included the Kingdom of Mali (circa 1200 to 1500 A.D.) with its famous commercial city of Timbuctoo.

In iron processing and other fields, this kingdom was the equal of European craftsmen of their time. Near the Gulf of Guinea, too, the Black Africans had created cultures which were regarded by the first Portuguese discoverers as on a par with those of Europe. Another was the Kingdom of the Congo, on both sides of the lower Congo. Similar kingdoms existed in East and South East Africa. Social development had not gained this high standard in all parts of Africa.

The first period of colonization: The independent development of Africa was stopped abruptly by colonial conquest. Slave traders came to deprive Africa of its most precious possession, its people. Slave-hunting and trading increased swiftly since the plantation owners in America, from the sixteenth century on, called for ever more new African manpower. (p. 8.)

At the Fifteenth General Assembly of the United Nations in 1960 the representatives of the imperialist states had to approve a "Declaration to Grant Independence to the Colonial Peoples and Countries." The first Article states: "The subjection of peoples to alien subjugation, domination and exploitation constitutes a denial of fundamental human rights, is contrary to the UN Charter, and is an impediment to the promotion of world peace and cooperation."

Although this declaration publicly condemned colonial rule the imperialist powers attempted to maintain at least part of their former possessions. In Algeria the Algerian National Liberation Front had to wage war against French colonial armies for seven years. Although these totaled almost a million mercenaries and police, equipped with modern weapons, who fought brutally, even against women and children, the desire for liberty of the Algerian people could not be crushed. In 1962 the French imperialists had to grant Algeria independence. It was shown once more that even the greatest military superiority is not enough to defeat a people which courageously fights for liberty and social progress.

A similar fight is taking place today in Angola, which the Portuguese colonialists hold on to as stubbornly as to their other African colony Mozambique. But they, too, cannot stop a development which history indicates will lead to the destruction of colonialism. (p. 70.)

Black slaves: The striking population contrasts in South Africa become, particularly clear in the mining city of Johannesburg.

Visitors notice first the huge new high-rise office buildings owned by industry and trade monopolies, the true rulers of city and state.

If you see the city from a skyscraper you notice huge mounds on the outskirts. They are the tips of forty gold mines. Underground work is done mainly by Blacks. At 800–1,000 or even 2,500 meters they work in stifling heat. They are paid two marks (70 cents) daily, a tenth of what a white worker gets. After work, they have to return to a barbed-wire enclosure which they may not leave.

Usually miners are hired for a year. If they do not renew their contract they must return to a reservation. These areas are clearly marked and they may not leave without certificates. Time and again their grinding poverty forces them to work in the mines." (p. 70.)

Segregation laws are approved by a white minority (Apartheid) and prove discrimination.

For example, Blacks are punished if in the streets after 9 p.m. If an African wants to go to another city he must have a permit from his employer showing the reason for the journey, etc. Africans may not use the same vehicles as whites.

Everywhere, in parks, cafes, and cinemas you read: "For Europeans Only."

The struggle of Africans for equality has led to many sacrifices. Not only the young African states but most other countries condemn this oppression. Among the few states with relations with South Africa are West Germany, whose ex-President Heinrich Lübke even described its racial policy as "ideal." West German monopolies increasingly participate in South African industry and thus directly in exploiting Africans. (p. 72.)

The cynicism of the U.S. ruling class is evident in the treatment of Negroes who get inferior jobs and a fraction of the wages white workers have won after struggles of the Unions. (p. 109.)

New York is a city of striking contrasts. It is marked on the one hand by huge office buildings of the monopolies, banks and insurance companies and the luxury districts of the ruling classes. On the other hand are slums, where most degrading conditions prevail. The Negro Harlem and East Side slums have won particular ill fame.

Slum dwellings have increased by 11,000 yearly; but, only 5,500 low-rent apartments were built. New York now has 400,000 slum dwellings ...

Over 800,000 New Yorkers are Black. Since most landlords do not rent to Negroes, most of these live in Harlem or other slums. (pp. 113–114.)

Cotton plantations were in the South, east of the Mississippi. Negro slaves did the field work. When slavery was banned 100 years ago, the landlords employed Negroes as badly-paid wage workers or rented them land in return for half their crops. There are such farms even today. But, after World War II, many left the countryside for the cities to look for factory jobs or work in service industries. (p. 128.)

From *Biology for the 10th Grade*, 16-year-olds, Berlin, 1968.

The Human Races Today

The development of races, like the origin of the species, is the result of the close interaction of various factors, of which the chief are the continually new combinations of inherited characteristics through sexual reproduction, development of new features through mutation, selection and isolation. In human beings, the process of isolation is influenced not only by the natural frontiers between the human communities, but also by reproduction barriers of social origin. Within the isolated spheres there are differing developments, which finally lead to differences in frequency and different combinations of varying inherited characteristics. Thus, there grow up at first local types and then, with longer periods of isolation of large areas, different races. Continually appearing mutations, changes in environment, the shift, change or abolition of old isolating barriers ensure changes within and between races. Therefore, these races are not final form groups, but only temporary, provisional products in the framework of continuous biological development. This is why we generally do not find all the characteristics of the race in a single individual.

Since all present-day humans can mutually fertilize, they all belong to one species, Homo sapiens. The various races of Homo sapiens can be assembled in groups: we recognize three such: Europoid, Mongoloid and Negroid. (pp. 74–75.)

At present, technical, cultural and social progress means that old isolating barriers are being overcome at increasing speed. This inevitably leads to a greater mixing of humanity, and probably at some date to the disappearance of anthropological racial differentiation. Investigations show that this process of race amalgamation is not disadvantageous since races vary in characteristics irrelevant to human existence. The only complications arising because of racial mixture, and which can be tragic for those concerned are based on senseless ideological and social prejudices which still play a great role in the U.S. and other capitalist countries. There are no biologically inferior or particularly valuable races. Variations in levels of civilization which still exist are social and not biological in origin. Racial arrogance has no scientific basis, and no one has the right to discriminate against, to oppress, persecute and still less kill another human because of the color of his skin as was done so inhumanly by fascism. Many human groups and even entire peoples were described by fascism as biologically inferior and treated accordingly simply because they hindered its imperialist aims. The pseudo-scientific racism of the "master race" brought unmeasured suffering to humanity—something which must never be allowed to happen again. (p. 76.)

These are remarkable examples of how to train youth to reject the poisons of racist ideology. If one looks back twenty-seven years and reads what Hitler was teaching the youth about the German "master race," and contrasts it with what is being taught in the G.D.R. today, then one can say: This, too, is one of the "miracles" of our time.

CHAPTER 10

The G.D.R., Vietnam and Africa

Developments with regard to the peoples of Vietnam, the G.D.R. and Cuba are unique in world history. Here, we find three small nations influencing world developments as never before. The roles they play are determined by the present epoch. They are anchored in the great power of the Socialist community headed by the Soviet people and other anti-imperialist forces. Together, these revolutionary currents represent the majority of mankind.

However, the people of Vietnam, the G.D.R. and Cuba, in their own way and with their limited material resources, have added greatly to the world revolutionary process. I shall, therefore, try to show in this chapter how the G.D.R. broke out of the world-wide capitalist economic and political blockade and was able greatly to influence the underdeveloped countries particularly in Africa.

One of the main factors is that the G.D.R. is a living example of how it is possible for small nations to achieve a rapid growth from their present limited economic status. In spite of obvious differences in the living conditions in Arab and African countries, a great deal can be learned from the G.D.R.'s experiences.

Another lesson to learn from the experiences of the G.D.R. is that the people are the main force that make history. Technology and science are vital, but the people are decisive.

Several years ago, the Black Panther Party in the U.S. coined the slogan, "Power to the People!" This was an attractive slogan but it had its limitations. Power is not something that is given to the people by an elitist force; it is something that a minority can stimulate the people to attain. A more correct slogan would be: "Power to and from the People!" A proper correlation of these two concepts is the basis for progress.

When one studies the achievements of the G.D.R. and observes its relations with other people, especially with the underdeveloped countries, what comes into focus is the role of the people. In internal matters, there is no process of refinement by the people there. This free flow between the leaders and the people is the key to their successes.

What is true of internal matters is equally true of foreign policy. Mobilization of the people for a proper understanding of foreign affairs has been decisive. Their role is determined by their knowledge of the objectives.

The G.D.R. has built a social system predicated upon undoing the harm done to the German image through two world wars. The objective was to establish cooperative and peaceful relations with all peoples. It is especially sensitive to the impact that Nazi Germany, with its "master race" ideology, has had upon the world and it is determined to help remove racism as a force in the world of today. This has been its objective from the very beginning.

In this respect we see two related developments: One by the government and the other by the people. The Ministry of Foreign Affairs, on March 21, 1971, marked the International Day of Struggle Against Racial Discrimination with the following statement:

> "Ever since its foundation, the G.D.R. has devoted special attention to the struggle against all forms of racial discrimination. The anti-Nazi and anti-racialist decisions of the anti-Hitler coalition have been carried out conscientiously in their entirety within her territory.
>
> "Thus, the G.D.R. has created all the guarantees —both socio-economic and juridical—to guarantee that racism and Nazism will never re-emerge in this country. The G.D.R.'s policy rests on the objectives and principles of the Charter of the United Nations and aims at equal cooperation with all peoples and races."
>
> ("Racial Oppression Must be Removed," *Foreign Affairs Bulletin*, No. 10/71; Berlin, G.D.R.)

The foreign policy as outlined in this Bulletin is not only the business of diplomats but also of the people. To support these objectives, there came into existence the G.D.R. League for Friendship Among the Peoples. It was founded in 1961 and is composed of 11 Friendship Societies and 76 other organizations. All these have contacts with partner organizations in foreign countries and maintain Cultural and Information Centers in a large number of countries. Over 100 foreign universities and scientific institutions have concluded direct Friendship Agreements with corresponding institutions in the G.D.R.

There is fundamental unity between people and government on international issues, and the government can be sure of popular support when it takes a stand against imperialist aggression or racist oppression.

On November 27, 1969, over 300,000 citizens joined in one of the largest demonstrations ever held in the history of Berlin, to express their indignation at the atrocities committed by the United States in Vietnam. Among the many speeches made that day, one was delivered by Albert Norden, a Member of the Politburo of the Central Committee of the SED:

> "Full of abhorrence and anger, the whole world accuses the main perpetrators of these war crimes. They are those forces which without a scruple make millions in profits out of the blood and tears of the Vietnamese people. The military intervention costs 100 million dollars every day and brings the American monopolists profits of 500 and more percent. The more Vietnamese are killed, the higher grow the profits of the all-powerful arms trusts . . . Who ever remains silent shares the guilt. Whoever today does not demand the immediate withdrawal of the American troops from Vietnam and the cessation of the ruthless bombing, makes himself an accomplice to the greatest crime of our time."

I was in the G.D.R. at the time this demonstration was planned, and I saw with "mine own eyes" the vastness of the preparations among the people. Everywhere I went, I saw posters and signs displaying the atrocities of the U.S. in Vietnam. I saw children, youth and women in the streets signing petitions, selling buttons and collecting money.

In addition to the supplies the G.D.R. has been sending to the Democratic Republic of Vietnam, the Friendship Societies have collected millions of Marks for medical and other aid. From 1965 to 1969, the people donated 240 million marks. The young miners produced 9,000 tons of potash fertilizer over their quota as a donation for Vietnamese farms. Over a million people have donated blood to save lives in Vietnam.

Trade with North Vietnam has increased greatly since 1965. Enterprises and universities in the G.D.R. have trained over 3,500 young Vietnamese to become specialists. In 1969 alone, the G.D.R. helped build or expand ten factories in North Vietnam.

Another instance of promoting international solidarity by the people has been the campaign to free Angela Davis. This campaign has aroused an entire people into action. One cannot walk the streets of a city in the G.D.R. without seeing evidence of the deep concern of the people. Posters of her are seen everywhere; protest postcards and petitions are in the streets, in schoolrooms, restaurants and everywhere one goes. The Women's Democratic Federation alone has collected over one and a half million signatures and has sent them to U.S. authorities, condemning the injustices done to this Black woman. Never in history has there been such a world-wide response for the defense of a Black woman, and the people of the G.D.R. have been foremost in this just cause.

As already stated, various G.D.R. organizations maintain direct relations with similar organizations in other countries. I once heard it said that when a society finds the key to unlock the hearts of the women, it finds the key to success in whatever they undertake to do. In the relations between the people of the G.D.R. and the African peoples, there is no better example of this than the relationship of the Women's Democratic Federation to similar organizations in Africa. This group maintains relations with people in over 80 countries, including 24 women's organizations in African countries. These include the "Conference of African Women" in South Africa (exile organization), Tanzania, Sierra Leone, Somalia, Sudan, Togo, Algeria, Angola, People's Republic of the Congo (Brazzaville), Dahomey, Guinea, Mauritius, Mozambique, Nigeria, Guinea-Bissau and Zambia.

Since 1965, delegates of ten women's organizations from the G.D.R. have visited African countries. Of great importance were the visits of the President of the Women's Democratic Federation, Mrs. Ilse Thiele, to Guinea, Mali and Tanzania. I consulted her about her experiences and she told me they had helped to develop and strengthen cooperation with the women's organizations of those countries. In most cases they have signed contracts of friendship, which define the nature of the cooperation.

Since that time also, delegations of twelve women's organizations have come to the G.D.R. from African countries. Seminars have also been held to discuss experiences in the work for the equality of women. Summing up, Mrs. Thiele stated:

> "Internationalism is firmly tied up in the thoughts and actions of our women. Their indignation and abhorrence are directed against the criminal, reactionary policies of the imperialists, expressed in the aggressions against the people of Indochina and the Near East and Africa, as well as in the suppression of those fighting for freedom and equal rights in the capitalist world ... The women confirm their affection for the victims of imperialist aggression by impressive solidarity actions for Vietnam, Laos and Cambodia, and for the Arab and African peoples."

There have been many responses from a number of important women's groups in Africa. One such is by Mrs. Odhiambo Odinga of Kenya:

> "It was particularly informative and important for me to see how in the G.D.R. the emancipation of women is practiced. I often spoke about my experiences in your country. Everywhere, my reports were received enthusiastically. For my countrymen, it is important to get the feeling of the hearty and friendly affection the women of the G.D.R. extended me. With them I felt as at home."
>
> (May 1965.)

What has been done by the Women's Democratic Federation is true of many other organizations, and especially of youth. The Free German Youth, for example, to show its international solidarity with African peoples has sent Youth Friendship Brigades to the underdeveloped countries. At the time of writing, there were one in Zanzibar, two in Guinea, two in Algeria, and two in Mali.

I discussed these brigades with Edwin Schroeder, in charge of one in Zanzibar. His brigade, he said, had the task of setting up an apprenticeship workshop. The tools, machines and equipment had been given to them by the government of the G.D.R. The young G.D.R. workers and experts set up the workshop and trained the young Africans. They not only trained them; they also lived together. They had discussions, joint social events, etc. Schroeder said he was pleased with this experience because the Africans looked upon him and his comrades as Africans among Africans, and emphasized: "It was not just a matter of someone coming in to train them, but friendly, mutual assistance."

The young workers from the G.D.R. also learned much. They saw for the first time the effects of imperialist policy in these former colonies, and they were shocked. Out of this contact, many came to feel real friendship for their African brothers and sisters, and hated imperialism even more.

An organization of great significance in maintaining contact and aiding the peoples of Africa is the German-African Society in the G.D.R. Its activities were dealt with in an interview with the head of the Society:

Question: How, in your opinion, can the German-African Society help inform the G.D.R. population even more about developments in Africa, and further strengthen solidarity with its peoples?

Minister Schulze: A great deal is already being done in the G.D.R., and we can say that the spirit of solidarity is firmly rooted in us. Concerning the activities of the German-African Society, we intend to lay still greater stress on keeping G.D.R. citizens informed about the national liberation movement and the problems of the emergent African states through lectures, discussions, exhibitions, the press, radio and television. Thus, the German-African Society helps the people give living expression to friendship with the African peoples. In doing this, the Society should rely still more on the help of our friends in Africa. We shall make 1970, the tenth anniversary of the great-Africa year, an occasion for increasing the activity of the German-African Society, and for consolidating the links with Africa.

Question: How will the German-African Society improve cooperation with the national friendship societies in Africa, and in what way can it support the African Liberation Movement?

Minister Schulze: We have joined efforts to put experience gained in the G.D.R. at the service of progress in Africa. We fight the common enemies of our peoples—imperialism, colonialism and neo-colonialism. We consider it our task to support the friendship societies in the African countries and their allies—the trade unions, women's and youth organizations, scientists and scholars—

and to inform people of Socialist construction in the German Democratic Republic. In addition, the German-African Society works closely with many organizations here and helps them train people who go to work in Africa as members of friendship labor teams, as teachers or other specialists. We distribute in Africa material for qualification and further education, especially among African graduates of G.D.R. colleges and universities. These activities of the German-African Society reflect the policy of our government—one of peace and understanding between peoples and of struggle against imperialism, racism, colonialism."

(The Task of the German-African Society in the G.D.R.: Strengthening Links with Africa, an Interview of Minister Rudolph Schulze, President of the German-African Society in the G.D.R., with Thomas Wedegartner.)

Generally, the people of the G.D.R. support the actions of their Government in support of the peoples in South Africa and the Portuguese colonies. An indication of the type of support given is related by an eyewitness of a Portuguese attack, as follows:

"My report would be one-sided if I did not also mention that the activities of the other German state, the German Democratic Republic, are notable in the free part of Mozambique.

"I visited an administrative center surrounded by huts, spread far apart in the bush. At a distance, at wide intervals made necessary by air raids, I saw the school complex—grass-covered huts for instruction, sometimes fenced-in areas without roofs, containing only logs for the children to sit on. There were also huts providing living accommodation for those children whose parents were at the front. School classes were taking place everywhere—some for children, some for adults. The adults often had a rifle next to their books. The exercise books in which the children write come from the G.D.R., as do the pencils. That is certainly no world-shaking act of solidarity. But the teachers told me that until recently they had to make do with dried cassava root as substitute chalk and charred wooden boards as a sort of slate. Indicating how he teaches the six-year-olds arithmetic—with little wooden sticks placed next to each other—one of them told me that this was a method introduced by a teacher from the G.D.R. who had worked for some time at the Mozambique Institute in Dar-es-Salaam.

"I found many such examples of the solidarity of the G.D.R. with the fighting population of Mozambique—ranging from clothing and aluminum utensils to woolen blankets and tents. Samora Machel told me: 'The G.D.R. is helping us morally, politically and materially as well. We value this here in the liberated areas especially. We look upon the G.D.R. not only as a friend but as our direct ally.'"

I was interested in knowing the economic relationship of the G.D.R. to the developing countries, so

I visited some of the leading professors at the University of Economic Science in Berlin. They said that the volume of help that the G.D.R. was able to give was limited in comparison with some other countries. However, whatever help they are giving is designed to end the division of labor which had existed in the days of direct imperialist controls, and defeat the present neo-colonialist policies. The latter aim at keeping the emerging nations of Africa and Asia in a permanent state of economic dependence, where these nations remain sources of raw material and a market for manufactured products. The professors explained to me that everything the G.D.R. does is designed to help change all that.

They stated they were training people both in their schools and in the former colonies to use modern machinery and equipment. They furnish much of the material for schools and laboratories in those countries. They have given much equipment for the transport system and the fishing industry, as well as exporting the types of equipment that will enable African and Asiatic people to build their own factories. The G.D.R. provides a market for the products from these plants, so the factory owners won't have to compete in the world market at a disadvantage.

I was also informed that interest rates on loans to developing countries are lower than those of the imperialists. The interest rate on loans made by the G.D.R. range from 2.5 percent to 3 percent, whereas the imperialist countries charge 4 to 6 percent. Repayment to the imperialist countries is generally due within 7 years; to the G.D.R., within 15.

Students coming from these countries to the G.D.R., I was told, receive monthly allowances of from 300 marks for undergraduates to 500 marks for post-graduates. They have good housing, free medical care and there is a special department at each university to handle their problems.

These examples, and many more that could be cited, show that a new relationship exists between the G.D.R. and African peoples. As a result of its attainments and this relationship the German Democratic Republic has increasingly been able to break down the strong walls of resistance to its recognition as a sovereign state.

The Federal Republic (West Germany) has intervened energetically all over Africa, making threats to break off trade relations with countries recognizing the G.D.R. What has happened in this respect in Africa is an exception in world affairs. Today, 29 countries recognize the G.D.R. Of these, 14 are in the Socialist community, as would be expected; and 11 are African countries.

As to the attitude of African peoples, I cite a few leading African personalities:

"As long as it was only the socialist countries, the Soviet Union, Rumania, etc. that took action against the Hallstein Doctrine, the West Germans had nothing to worry about. In every developing country they employed an arsenal of evasions and threats to discriminate against the German Democratic Republic.

"The economically underdeveloped African

states are still being blackmailed by the West German government. Although the G.D.R. has trade representations, as well as Consulates-General in Africa, the imperialist powers still attempt in every way to divert Africa's attention from the irrefutable fact of the existence of two German states. The news that Iraq, Syria, the U.A.R., Cambodia, Southern Yemen and the Sudan had granted diplomatic recognition to the G.D.R. spread like wildfire in Africa. Uncle Hallstein and his masters must have had headaches, for this recognition signified to them that they had invested large sums of money in a useless project. The courageous step taken by these countries certainly gave Kiesinger and Brandt an attack of political diarrhea.

"It is, indeed, very difficult to shut one's eyes to facts. Whether one wants it or not, the sun shines dispersing the swadows of darkness, as it has done in the G.D.R. The G.D.R. is Africa's lucky star. We, in Africa, are aware of this."

(Dr. H. K. Matipa, Zambia, "The Grave of the Hallstein Doctrine," April 1970.)

At a Friendship Week in Nigeria, Dr. Tygliyele, Dean of the Faculty of Education in Lagos, stated:

"The victory of the Soviet Union and the Allied Powers over Hitler fascism confronted the German people with a real opportunity and necessity of abolishing once and for all the reactionary power of imperialism and militarism, and to set out on the road to peace and social progress. In the eastern part of Germany, now the German Democratic Republic, that opportunity and obligation was accepted by the people under the leadership of the working class. The new and favorable historical conditions provided a sound foundation for the new experiment.

"G.D.R. policy in Europe and the world has been that of peaceful co-existence, support for the national liberation movements of Asia, Africa and Latin America."

("Friendship Week in Nigeria," p. 27.)

He further stated:

"During the crisis and the war to crush Ojukwu's secession, the G.D.R., the Soviet Union and other Socialist countries supported the cause of Nigerian unity. In contrast, the German Federal Republic, France and other imperialist sources supported Ojukwu with arms and finance."

This exception of the situation on the African Continent is also pointed out by a British writer, David Childs, in a book on East Germany:

"Nor does the list of countries in which the G.D.R. is represented ... reveal the full extent of East German influence abroad. For example, in Algeria, Tanzania, Ghana and the U.A.R., more persons are assigned to the G.D.R. Missions than to the respective Embassies of the Federal Republic."

East Germany, Frederick A. Praeger, Inc., New York, 1969, p. 256.)

These developments prove conclusively that racism is not inherent in man and that, on German soil where it had been drilled so ruthlessly into the minds of the people, a new generation has arisen which consciously rejects it. Taking in their totality, we see that the people of the G.D.R. stand for peace and friendship among the peoples, that it is an invaluable force working for the freedom of all humankind.

The people of the G.D.R. drew the lessons that Gerhart Eisler, Albert Norden and Albert Schreiner called for when at the end of World War II they wrote:

> "If the overwhelming majority of Germans draw up a balance sheet of their history . . . If they recognize the victories of the United Nations armies . . . as national victories . . . If they look upon the victories of the Nazi armies as themes for national mourning—Then will a new nation be born, then finally will come the day in which the Germans will use their . . . talents in the service of peaceful human progress . . . Only then will German misery come to an end . . . only then will the name of Germany cease to be identical with bestiality; only then will the Germans become a people who have ceased for all time to represent a horrible nightmare to the peoples of the world." (*Lessons of Germany*, International Publishers, New York, 1945, p. 219.)

PART III

The Bonn Government and Racism

CHAPTER 11

The Betrayal of the Potsdam Agreement in West Germany

Before the close of World War II, many people all over the world had hoped that the war-making potential of the German nation would be destroyed. They were determined that never again would German militarism constitute a threat to the peace of the world.

Especially were they concerned with removing from power all forces in the Nazi war machine. This meant not only the elimination of political personalities, but the Junkers, the monopolists, the Nazi teachers, as well as the jurists who had condemned thousands to death, and especially those responsible for the horrors of the concentration camps.

These views were not only those of the people in the Allied countries, but also of the German people. They were expressed in no uncertain terms not only in the Eastern zone but also in the Western zone where the Allied Powers were in control. We have already discussed the situation in the Eastern zone where a plebiscite showed a big majority for the nationalization of plants owned by the monopolies. This trend was also evident in the Western zone. For example, Article 41 of the Constitution of the West German Land of Hesse was confirmed in a plebiscite, but the U.S. occupation authorities prevented it from being carried out.

It read:

> "To be transformed into collective property are: the mining industry (coal, potash, ores), iron and steel-producing plants, power plants, railway and air transport. Large banks and insurance institutions are to be administered by the State."

At that time, the Works-Council Chairman of Krupp, Vereinigte Stahlwerke, Mannesmann, Haniel, Hoesch and Klöckner, and other huge monopoly groupings unanimously adopted resolutions calling for conversion of these concerns into state property.

In December 1945, the Land Parliament of Lower Saxony called for the nationalization of the petroleum industry.

On August 6, 1948, the Land Parliament of North Rhine-Westphalia adopted a law on the nationalization of the Ruhr coal mines. In the Rhineland-Palatinate, a law created the possibility of turning into social property the coal, potash and ore-mining concerns, the metallurgical industry, and the power and transport systems. Similar laws were introduced in Baden-Wurttemberg and Bavaria.

Even Dr. Kurt Schumacher, then chairman of the West German Social-Democratic Party, who earned a heavy burden of guilt for his bitter hostility to the unity of the German working class, declared at the party congress of the SPD in Nuremberg on June 29, 1947:

> "We face the task of destroying the power of the remaining clique of capitalism which has led to the devastation of Europe. They and their mode of thinking are no longer subject to correction. It

178

is necessary to say Yes or No to them. If one says Yes, one becomes culpable. It is also impossible to buy facilities to be socialized from the gentlemen of the coal, iron, steel, chemicals, power, cement and mineral resources."

The West German Trade Union Federation, the DGB, at its founding on October 14, 1949, in Munich, proclaimed as its major goal: Turning the key industries into collective property, as well as the socialization of the mining industry, the iron and steel industry, the important transport facilities and credit institutions. In the founding document, it is further declared that the

> "... economic intention and the management demand central national planning, so that private self-interest does not triumph over the needs of the over-all economy."

Even the Ahlen economic program of the West German Christian Democratic Union (CDU), the party of Adenauer, in February 1946, was unable to ignore the demand of the overwhelming majority in the east and the west to expropriate the large capitalist concerns which were responsible for and benefited from the Second World War. The CDU went even further than the Potsdam Agreement. The Ahlen program states:

> "The capitalist economic system has not been adequate for the vital state and social interests of the people. After the terrible political, economic and social collapse which was the result of a crim-

inal policy of power politics, only an order that is new from the ground up can follow. The content and goal of the new order can no longer be the capitalist aspirations for profit and power but only the well-being of our people."

Karl Arnold, the CDU Prime Minister of North Rhine-Westphalia, defined the Ahlen program in a government declaration to the Land Parliament on June 17, 1947, as follows:

"The previously one-sided power structure in the big industries will be abolished and the creation of such structures in the future will be prevented by the fact that the German raw materials industries (coal, iron and steel-producing, as well as the large chemical concerns which dominate the market monopolistically) are to be turned into collective property. Participation of large-scale private capital in such plants will be ruled out."

Naturally, these programmatic declarations of the party of big capital were only treacherous maneuvers to mislead the people. But the fact that even the CDU was forced to resort to such maneuvers and to declare itself in agreement with the Potsdam Agreement clearly shows what the mood was among the mass of CDU's followers. There was literally nobody who dared openly to identify himself with the capitalist system. The crimes of the German imperialists against the peoples were too great, as was also their guilt before the German people.

Under the impact of developments such as these, the

Allies met in Potsdam and signed a declaration on August 2, 1945 providing a program to eliminate the possibility of a third world war emanating from German soil.

We have already noted the fact that, in the Soviet-occupied zone, now the G.D.R., the provisions of the Potsdam Agreement were faithfully adhered to.

But this was not the case in the Western zone, the Federal Republic of Germany, which was under the command of the Western Allied Powers. The violation of the Potsdam Agreement in West Germany was also a violation of the right of self-determination of the German people, the right to deal adequately with their own war-makers.

What are some of the reasons behind the betrayal of the Potsdam Agreement? They are rooted in the politics of the twentieth century. They are based on two major contradictions.

On the one hand, prior to the outbreak of World War I, the struggle was for a re-division of world markets, of colonies, among the major powers. Coming into the twentieth century, most markets and colonies had already been divided up. A life and death struggle ensued for these markets.

On the other hand, the imperialist powers were confronted with the October Revolution in Russia—a contradiction between capitalism and socialism, in addition to the contradictions among the imperialist powers themselves.

And it had been mainly the interplay of these two contradictions which has been the root of wars and preparations for wars in this century.

Between the two world wars, Germany was viewed as a buffer zone between the major imperialist powers and the new Socialist state.

This was why Hitler was permitted to come to power, to scrap the Versailles Treaty and to rebuild his war potential. Indeed, he was aided in this process by the Western powers, who later were compelled to go to war against him.

This was the meaning of the Munich Agreement of 1938. The aim of Britain was to give him a free hand to attack the U.S.S.R. This was why Hitler was allowed to destroy the Popular Front Government in Spain.

The Grand Coalition which defeated Hitler in World War II was not what was wanted by the Western powers. They would have preferred a war between the Soviet Union and Germany, a war in which both would become weak. However, Hitler did not follow the tactical pattern desired by the ruling circles of Britain, France and the United States.

He made his initial assault upon France. When Hitler's Wehrmacht had overrun much of Europe, British and American policy-makers became convinced that they had to unite with a major enemy, the Soviet Union, in order to destroy Hitler.

But throughout the war, many in the British and American ruling circles felt that this was the wrong war; and if it had to be fought this way, then they would pursue it in a way that both the competing German imperialism and Soviet Communism would be wiped out or greatly weakened.

This view was expressed by Harry S. Truman, who

later became President of the United States. In the *New York Times* of June 24, 1941, he stated:

> "When we see that Germany is winning, we should help Russia; and when Russia wins, we should help Germany. Let as many as possible kill each other off."

This was also the guiding thought of Winston Churchill, who consistently sabotaged the opening of a Second Front.

So, while the Western powers had to unite with the Soviet Union in a war that was basically anti-fascist, they nevertheless retained their hope of destroying both enemies. Many people in the ruling circles of the U.S. participated in the Grand Anti-Fascist Coalition with the dream of furthering American domination of the world. They did not conceal their views but announced them under the slogan, "The next half of the 20th Century will be the American Century."

Henry A. Wallace, then Vice-President of the U.S., sought to counteract this slogan by saying, "The next half of the 20th Century will be the Century of the Common Man."

However, the viewpoint expressed by Wallace was not the dominant one. The big American monopolists, before the war's end, made all the necessary preparations to enter a world torn by wartime devastation and to reorganize its economy largely under their control.

Thus, the American monopolists fought World War II essentially for the same thing Hitler did—namely, world domination.

Consequently, at the war's end, these people were not prepared to carry out the provisions of the Potsdam Agreement, since this would have allowed a condition to exist where the people might put an end to imperialism in general.

During the war and at its close, they prepared to achieve what they had been fighting for. Thus, the Cold War was launched by Truman and Churchill in 1946. Under these conditions, West Germany was to be rebuilt as an instrument of Anglo-American foreign policy.

What the Allied Powers did in the Western zone is best described by Germans. Let us take the reactions of a German woman, typical of most Germans:

> "You Americans go to extremes. Of course there are still Nazis and neo-Nazis. It would be as foolish to deny that as to say that all Germans were Nazis, when, in fact, thousands died and suffered torture in camps or lived in fear of death.
>
> "At the end of the war, posters in Germany proclaimed haughtily that you Americans had come as conquerors. We were told that we Germans had committed more crimes against humanity than any other nation in history... Our surrender, don't forget, was an unconditional one, on your terms.
>
> "But it wasn't long before you had differences with your wartime allies. Soon, to get support for the Western cause, you turned to us. German monopolists were given the nod to rebuild their

industries. Soon you told us to start a new army ... You pardoned some of the same war criminals you told us you were going to hang. Some of them have gained top positions in German political and industrial life, while others draw fat pensions at taxpayers' expense.

"... We're still paying out millions each year in reparations and restitution to Jews and other victims of the Nazi terror; but the terrorists are collecting other millions in form of pensions. Just what do you expect?"
(John Dornberg, *Schizophrenic Germany*, Macmillan, New York, 1961, p. 6.)

Delbert Clark, a war veteran, went back to Germany as a journalist two years after the war and wrote about the new Germany, as follows:

"Millions of Americans believed, when World War II ended, that this time they could really hope for peace. Millions of others were convinced that if there was a remaining threat, it was the threat of the Soviet Union. Only a handful foresaw that their own government, yielding on the one hand to the pressure of business-as-usual, and on the other hand to the German argument that her defeat had created an intolerable political vacuum which must be quickly filled if we were not to have war with Russia, would adopt a policy calculated to negate all the principles for which we had fought the war."
(Delbert Clark, *Again the Goose Step*, Bobbs-Merrill Co., New York, Foreword.)

And further, he wrote:

"We came back to New York after nearly two years in post-war Germany, and we were sad and angry. We were both war veterans, my wife and I, and we both had cherished the hope, almost the belief, that Germany, at least, would not again be permitted to tear the civilised world asunder . . .

"Then we went to Germany. We found many instances of the 'old Guard' filtering back into positions of influence."
(Ibid. p. 15.)

Disillusionment over the failure to carry out the Potsdam Agreement disturbed many people in the West. Among them was Lord Russell, who had been a member of the British prosecuting team at Nuremberg. He wrote:

"The occupying powers were intent on ridding Germany of all dangerous Nazis and ensuring that they would never again be active . . . The Yalta and Potsdam agreements had stated that one of the main objectives of the occupation must be 'the political purification of Germany.'

"In actual practice, however, the denazification program proved to be very little short of a farce."
(Lord Russell, *Return of the Swastika?*, David McKay Co., Inc., New York, 1969, p. 15.)

Lord Russell further states:

"In Bavaria, the *New York Times* reported, the re-employment in Government service of former active Nazis was more general and more open than elsewhere ... with State approval. The rumble of a protest began to sound. 'Today,' it was being said, 'we who were against Nazism and its philosophy are accused of being Nazis. The former Nazis are back in their positions and we are the public fools.' ...

"... Actually, as the *Times* pointed out, ... of a total of 20,682 civil servants who had belonged to the NSDAP or to parties affiliated to it, no less than 14,443 of them 'had been dismissed from party activities and later reinstated' ... By December 1949, more than 20 percent of the mayors in Bavaria were proven active Nazis ... "Control by former Nazis was not limited to the administration. The press in Bavaria, the *New York Times* further pointed out, also 'showed a Nazi trend' and 'more than 90 newspapers were, in 1949, owned and edited by the same men' who had run them during the Third Reich.

(*Ibid.* pp. 19–20.)

On October 26, 1946, the *Saturday Evening Post* reported that, of 361 top steel executives who were Nazis, only 33 had been arrested, and the rest were still in their old jobs. The *New York Times* of April 30, 1949 reported that an investigating committee of the U.S. War Department had decided that no large monopoly association in West Germany had suffered.

(From D. N. Pritt, *Unrepentant Aggressors*, Lawrence and Wishart, London, 1969, p. 26.)

It is well-documented that the main forces behind the Third Reich were the big monopolies and armament industrialists, and yet they were the least touched in the postwar world. Most of those convicted got only minimal sentences. Today, those chiefly responsible for the Nazi war crimes—the directors of I.G. Farben, Flick, Krupp and others—are still among the most powerful people in West Germany.

Perhaps the best illustration of the betrayal of the Potsdam Agreement is what happened to Alfried Krupp, head of a trust which has been a main force behind Germany's war-making potential. He was sentenced to twelve years in prison and his property confiscated. Three years later (January 31, 1951), U.S. High Commissioner McCloy reviewed sentences against leading war criminals. Three days later, Krupp and his ten directors were in civilian clothes, and subsequently had all of the property returned. Krupp died a few years ago, still one of the richest men in the world.

Thus, the Federal Republic of Germany is a country in which several thousand millionaires hold economic and political power to a greater degree than ever before in German history.

In July 1965, the German Democratic Republic released *The Brown Book*, which sent shock waves all over the world. It contains the most complete documentation of the men who today make policy in the Federal Republic. It published the Nazi dossiers which recorded the activities of thousands of former Nazis and the crimes to which they had been accomplices. This documentation was a vast extension of the disclosures during the Nuremberg Trials. It revealed that those with criminal Nazi backgrounds included: the Federal President; 20 Ministers and State Secretaries of the Federal Republic; 189 generals and admirals of the Bundeswehr in leading NATO positions, or officials of the Defense Ministry; 1,118 high judicial officials, public prosecutors and judges; 244 leading officials of the Foreign Office, Bonn Embassies and Consulates; 300 high officers of the Police Force and the Office for the Protection of the Constitution, as well as similar bodies. (The *Brown Book*, Executive Council of the National Front of Democratic Germany, Berlin, 1965, p. 15.)

T. H. Tetans, an American who studied the situation, declared:

> "After World War II, Washington, in great haste, transformed our former enemy into a close ally. The State Department called the approach to the new Germany 'a policy of calculated risk...' Once before, we tried a similar experience when America helped rebuild a strong Germany after the First World War, and almost overnight that 'reformed Germany of Weimar' was replaced by the Third Reich of Adolf Hitler."
>
> (T. H. Tetans, *The New Germany and the Old Nazis*, Random House, New York, 1961, p. 252.)

The evidence of a betrayal in the Western zone of Germany was so overwhelming that even Adenauer was forced to admit it. In the Bundestag debate of October 23, 1952, he admitted that 66 percent of the diplomats in higher positions were former Nazis, but he added that he "could not build up a foreign office without relying on such skilled men." (Ibid. p. 7.)

As *The Brown Book* indicated, these men were among the most atrocious murderers in history, and they were allowed by Adenauer and the Allied Powers to continue their work.

What have been some of the consequences of the betrayal of the Potsdam Agreement by the Allied Powers? They resulted in the return to power in West Germany of a force which constitutes the main threat to peace in Europe. They created a situation where anti-Semitism still flourishes. They led to fascist-like measures against the democratic rights of the people. They laid the basis for the continuation of Hitler's racist policies and subversive activities against the peoples of Africa. They left a menace to the future security and well-being of all of the people of the world.

Today, there is in West Germany a military force which is the focal point of the war danger in the heart of Europe. In 1955, the Western Allies brought the Federal Republic into NATO. A year after joining NATO, the Bonn Government introduced universal compulsory military service. Today, its Bundeswehr is the largest European army in NATO. It has 500,000 men armed with the most modern weapons, including carriers for nuclear weapons. In the various military staffs of NATO, West German officers are increasingly taking over more command posts. Thus, German militarism has been revived and not destroyed as provided for in the Potsdam Agreement.

It is well known that officers—former Nazis—have

played a part in the development and growth of a neo-Nazi party, the NPD. This party in 1969, twenty-four years after the Potsdam Conference, was able to obtain 1,400,000 votes in a federal election. It succeeded in winning representation in a number of Land Parliaments and in obtaining more votes in all than Hitler had received three years before he came to power. The neo-Nazi party is being promoted by the West German capitalists and the military in order to have fascist forces in reserve in case of need. The NPD continues to operate freely, while left-wing protest forces have been banned.

As a result of the Nazi propaganda, anti-Semitism is still prevalent in the Federal Republic. At various times in the last twenty years, it has assumed alarming proportions. In May 1959, *Look* published a story by its European editor, Edward M. Cory, entitled "Hitlerism in 1959." This article was in response to a large number of anti-Semitic outbursts. Cory pointed out:

> "For the past few months, it has been almost impossible to open a serious West German newspaper without finding some reference to anti-Semitism. Local law enforcement officials, instead of making every effort to combat these occurrences of racial hatred . . . were, in most cases, remiss in their duties."

Cory's article was based upon a number of developments which had taken place between Christmas Eve 1959 and January 28, 1960, when 685 anti-Semitic incidents were registered by police in West Germany. These were touched off by the smearing of swastikas and anti-Jewish slogans on the Cologne Synagogue, arson attempts on the Synagogue, Jewish School and the home of a Jewish citizen. Children and youth were involved in many of these incidents. According to the Federal Government's *White Book*, about 215 incidents involved children. John Dornberg says about this:

> "It seems illogical that an anti-Semitic movement could grow anew in a country where the Jews represent only 0.5 per cent of the population. Some 30,000 Jews in a country of 60 million simply don't have enough impact on the society to incite anti-Semitic activity. At least it would appear so, unless one stops to recall the unbelievable hatred which served as the basis for the mass extermination and expulsion of all Germany's Jews. The 30,000 who remain, or have returned, are merely the remnants, the flotsam and jetsam of modern history's most extensive and most brutal inquisitions."
>
> (John Dornberg, *Schizophrenic Germany*, Macmillan Co., New York, 1951, p. 170.)

Yes, it is unbelievable that such a situation would still exist. But, then, one must see that it is a logical consequence of the anti-Semitic propaganda which is permitted to continue in the F.R.G. During the events between the period already noted, there appeared slogans such as, "Down with the Jews!" "To the Gas Chambers!"—and they were thrown into taverns and houses owned or occupied by Jews. Anonymous letters were sent to employers demanding that all Jews in their employ be dismissed, and threatening telephone calls were received by many Jews.

A highlight of this new wave of anti-Semitism is found in Lord Russell's account of the Zind affair:

> "In 1957, the Zind affair took place. Its background begins with the war when a Jew named Kurt Lieser (he was in fact, half-Jewish but was classed as non-Aryan under the Nuremberg Laws) was sent to the concentration camp at Sulz and miraculously escaped the gas chamber during 'the Final Solution.' He had lived in Offenburg, and after the defeat of Germany, he very unwisely decided to return there. But he and his family were not accepted by the other inhabitants; they were more or less ostracized.
>
> "One evening, coming home from work rather later than usual, Lieser decided to dine out in the Zohringer Hof. After eating, he remained at the table to drink beer and read his newspaper. He was soon joined by another man of the town, Ludwig Zind, a teacher at the Grimmelshausen Gymnasium and quite a local celebrity. They entered into a conversation which soon degenerated into a brawl because of Zind's typically Nazi denunciation of Jews. The incident was to cause a sensation throughout the civilized world.
>
> "Although Zind was well known and the brawl was the talk of the town, no mention of it appeared in the local newspaper. But, somehow, it came to the notice of a correspondent of *Der Spiegel*. In December 1957, an article appeared

in that paper under the heading 'Israel Should Be Eradicated,' in which much of the conversation between Zind and Lieser was repeated: . . .

"Lieser: 'You as a teacher should feel ashamed of yourself. I suspect that you would even have the audacity to praise the Nazi mass murder.'

"Zind: 'In my opinion, far too few Jews went into the gas chambers.'

"Lieser: 'This is outrageous! Do you know that I spent the war in a concentration camp, that I was tortured and beaten and that I almost lost my voice?'

"Zind: 'What? That means they forgot to gas you, too? It is a pity that you did not go up in smoke like the others.'

"Lieser: 'Today you would put me in a concentration camp if you had your way, wouldn't you?'

"Zind: 'Why not? And let me add this: I would not hesitate to kill you!'

"Lieser: 'And what about my wife? Would you gas her, too?'

"Zind: 'Of course, I would! It could all be done at the same time.'

"Lieser: 'And what would you do with my two children?'

"Zind: 'For my part, they could stay alive, but let me tell you this: I am proud

that during the war I and my men
killed hundreds of Jews with shovel
blows on the skull. I would not
hesitate to do it again.'

"Lieser then jumped at Zind's throat calling him
a murderer, and Zind spat out, 'You dirty Jew!'"
(Lord Russell, *Return of the Swastika?*, David
McKay, New York, 1969, pp. 58–60.)

Such outbursts come mainly from people indoctrinated in anti-Semitism under Hitler. However, if that
were all that it represents, the problem would not be
so great because sooner or later the generation reared
under Hitler will depart from this earth. But what is
more alarming is that anti-Semitic and Nazi propaganda is in both open and veiled forms and continues
to exist in the Federal Republic. The Potsdam Agreement provided that:

> *German education shall be so controlled as to
> completely eliminate Nazi and militarist doctrines
> and to make possible the successful development
> of democratic ideas.*

It also provided that all Nazi and militarist activity
be prevented.

In the early postwar years, efforts were made in
some parts of the country to establish a genuinely
progressive system of education, but these were soon
abandoned. However, even such feeble attempts were
ineffective, since the entire teaching staff was left in-
tact.

By March 31, 1956, 181,282 Nazis had been

brought into various branches of government service, including teachers who had propagated anti-Semitism in universities and other schools. There are scores of Nazis who have written books, articles, etc., justifying Hitler's plans for world domination, racism, anti-Semitism, etc.

In most textbooks now in use, the Nazi crimes are not recounted at all and, if discussed, are played down until the picture is entirely false. The loss of the war is explained away in order to save the prestige of the military. The failure to win the war is attributed to bad preparation, and even bad luck! Such is the nature of the educational system.

With this type of propaganda in the classroom, it is easy to understand why so many young children participated in anti-Semitic outbursts during 1960 and 1961. Of late, there have not been any similar outbursts, but in the face of continued anti-Semitic propaganda such things are likely to re-occur.

Another development which was a consequence of the Potsdam betrayal was the re-emergence of fascist-like attacks upon the democratic liberties of the people. These were highlighted by what is now known as the *Spiegel* affair, and the subsequent adoption of a number of Emergency Decrees. On the night of October 26, 1962, the police converged on the Hamburg and Bonn offices of the political magazine *Der Spiegel*. The files and the archives of its Hamburg central office were impounded and three members of the editorial staff arrested. The publisher could not be located, but he turned himself in the following day. An associated editor and his wife were vacationing in Spain.

In the early hours of October 27 they were awakened by the Spanish police and arrested.

What was behind these raids? It was the contention of the Bonn Government that the magazine has printed confidential information from governmental files and, in so doing, had committed acts of treason. The article in question was called "The Foertsch Article," which claimed that detailed information had been presented by Franz Josef Strauss, Defense Minister, in which he had called for a massive step-up in German military preparations, including arming Germany with nuclear weapons.

The article also claimed that the West German Defense Ministry was considering two alternatives: an armed force of 580,000 men, costing annually 20 billion German marks; and to be armed with medium-range missiles, which would cost 23 billion marks, and according to the plan, the Bundeswehr would be increased to 750,000 troops.

The revelations of these plans startled people in Germany and the rest of the world. The raid and the imprisonment of the editors of *Der Spiegel* not only revealed that powerful and sinister forces—former Nazis—had made gigantic steps forward in preparation for another major war, but also showed the tremendous anti-war and pro-democratic feelings among the German people. There was an immediate protest all over West Germany. Students and faculty members demonstrated their opposition. Eventually the press was compelled to take a stand. This situation finally resulted in the resignation of Strauss and a pledge by Adenauer that he would retire following the next election. The *Spiegel* affair and the protest wave that followed played an important role in the eventual break-up of the CDU-dominated government which governed West Germany up until 1969.

Notwithstanding these developments, the *Spiegel* affair was preceded by legislation which even now has the potential of creating an open fascist dictatorship in the Federal Republic. In 1961, a number of Emergency Laws were drafted. These provided for a small group of about thirty persons to constitute themselves into an Emergency Parliament. They would be given the power of conscripting all males for military and defense work, conscripting private cars and other private property; prohibiting strikes, freezing all citizens on jobs or transferring them from one job to another at the will of the government; the tapping of telephones, postal censorship, etc. In other words, plans for a fascist dictatorship in times of peace. These laws were passed in the summer of 1968, 16 million voters defeated the coalition of political parties represented by Adenauer and Strauss. The people expressed their disapproval of the administrations of Adenauer and Kiesinger.

Power was placed in the hands of an alliance of the Social Democrats and a small liberal party, the Free Democrats. They were entrusted with the task of reversing the trends of the last quarter of a century.

Will they prove adequate to the task? That will depend entirely upon the alertness of the people of the West German Republic and the peoples of the world. The new government has concluded agreements with the Soviet Union and Poland, but there are still many inconsistencies in the policies of the Brandt Government. This is evident in its attitude toward the war in Vietnam and toward the African peoples. Racist propaganda against Black people continues in the Federal Republic and the subversive activities of the Bonn Government against the peoples on the African Continent have been stepped up, at the same time that Willy Brandt talks about peace and security in Europe.

CHAPTER 12

Racist Indoctrination in West Germany

Among the consequences of the restoration to power of former Nazis is the continued racist indoctrination of the people by the government. Quotations from the writings and speeches and textbooks written by these people are taken primarily from West German sources. Beginning with Wilhelm Groteluschen, this "Western" professor was one of the most important colonial pedagogues under fascism and, today, is still writing on Africa in West German textbooks (Hinrichs Lehrbuchreihe). Back in the Nazi days in 1936 he published in the *Zeitschrift für Erdkunde*:

- We need the colonies firstly for economic reasons.
- We need raw materials for our industry.
- We need markets for the products of that industry.

(Groteluschen, Wilhelm, "Main Points for Dealing With the German Colonies in Schools," published in *Zeitschrift für Erdkunde*, 4th annual volume, 1936, No. 17/18, p. 808.)

The Nazi Groteluschen stressed the colonial claims of fascism:

It is a matter of course for the schools passionately to canvass for German colonialism so as to help to propagate it as widely as possible among the whole people.

(Ibid. p. 804.)

Groteluschen wrote:

> Never would the Negro on his own be able to lay out a plantation. The long-term planning and scientific work of the white man is needed ... Physical work, however ... he cannot perform in the tropical climate. That only the Negro can do. The white man is the master doing the intellectual work, he is the supervisor and manager, the Negro is his servant and worker.
>
> (*Hinrichs Erdkundebuch für höhere Schulen*–Geography Textbook for secondary schools–1939, pp. 39–41.)

This Nazi textbook was republished after the war in West Germany. In the 1958 edition (pp. 34–35) this paragraph has been revised as follows:

> Never would the Negro be able to lay out a plantation on his own account. The long-term planning and scientific work of the white man is needed. Physical work, however, he cannot perform in the tropical climate. That he must leave to the Negro. The white man does the intellectual work, he has the control and management. He has to check everywhere.

An even more far-reaching adaptation can be found in the 1961 edition (p. 29):

> Through long-term planning and scientific work of the white man the African territories were greatly advanced economically ... Either voluntarily or forced the Africans did the physical work ... The white man only controlled and managed.

The basic racist ideas, however, in all variations have remained the same.

A West German paper slandered the national ensembles from Dahomey and the Cameroons touring West Germany in 1964:

> "Formerly such groups performed in zoos, at colonial exhibitions, at a panopticon, or in a circus. A photograph from the very beginning of this century promises '20 savage women from Dahomey.' Today they are the "Dahomey National Ensemble."
>
> (*Neues Afrika*, Bonn, October 1964, p. 358.)

After the performance of the "Ballet Africana" from Guinea, in West Berlin, a student paper wrote: "Is this not all too alien, savage, barbaric?" (*Colloquium*, West Berlin, October 9, 1962, p. 3.)

Taken from West German sources examples of racism follow:

> The Jordanien student Fayez Jaber worked in a Hamburg coffee firm until they fired him: "Go home, you Arab skunk!" (*Hamburger Morgenpost*, March 19, 1965.)

> A landlady in Cologne demanded from an Egyptian trainee an extra 20 marks in addition to the already high rent, remarking: "This is for the bed linen. It will be stained because you are a Black . . ." (*Neue Rheinzeitung*, Düsseldorf, August 13, 1964.)

> The Nigerian engineering student Ayemi, after a long search for a room, thought he had found one. He heard the neighbors say: "We shall try to get

that Black out." (*Frankfurter Allgemeine Zeitung*, April 9, 1964.)

At a discussion in Cologne: "The Blacks should climb the trees outside, then we shall have more room here." (*Frankfurter Rundschau*, February 4, 1963.)

In West Berlin, a gang of teenagers attacked a student from Chad: They demanded a cigarette from the Black man. When he did not comply, one of the gang knocked him down. Then all the rowdies beat and kicked him. He suffered injuries in the face, knee and thigh. The African had just arrived in Berlin. (*Telegraf*, West Berlin, June 22, 1962.)

These slanders are not isolated cases. They reflect the basic attitude in Bonn. An observer of the Bonn Government turned up at the 18th UN General Assembly and distributed a note which read as follows: "All (the students) can testify that the allegation about a revival of racist madness in the Federal Republic is untrue." (*Neues Afrika*, Bonn, Jan., 1964, p. 32.)

Let African students, bear witness to what they experienced in the Federal Republic.

A young Egyptian, for instance, reported about his bitter experience which also goes for many foreign students in West Germany:

"At the restaurant where I eat the proprietor said: 'Don't take it too seriously that you are Black.' Back home I would have hit him in the face. Here the papers would have written: 'German attacked by Arab.' So I just left without a word, although he had offended me and my people. I shall never forget it.

(*Kulturarbeit*, Cologne, January 1962, from the article "Foreign Students Study with us" by Dr. W. Rieger.)

Young trade unionists studying in the Federal Republic were treated as second class.

"Two Africans reported to journalists that their patience had come to an end. Time and again 'Negro' had been called after Africans. In trams passengers moved away from them. Several Africans had been turned out of a Duisburg restaurant."

(*Süddeutsche Zeitung*, Munich, October 29, 1962.)

And this is what some young Africans tell about discrimination against them:

Jean Mideda, Congo: "An elderly gentleman touched my face, then looked at his hand and called 'Nigger' after me."

Maurice Boucard, Chad: "At a dance the German girls refused to dance with us. And one of the German 'cavaliers' said to me: 'You are dirty. Move away a bit.'"

Dominique Bouhouyi, Congo: "At the laundry they write only 'Negro.'"

They always felt "the fear of the 'black man,' the feeling of being but an exhibit at a museum." (*Westfälische Rundschau*, Dortmund, October 26, 1962, from the article by Horst Behrend, "African Officials state: The Federal Republic has disappointed us.")

Prejudices endorsed by West German policy also exist among students. At a discussion in Frankfurt of the Union of Students from Angola, students told "about the 15-hour working day of forced laborers, illiteracy and the high infantile mortality. They depicted the liberation struggle in which over 50,000 were killed. The first German speaker alleged their report had been drafted 'somewhere else.' Africans who had bitterly accused the Salazar regime had to hear speakers say they were ungrateful." (*Frankfurter Rundschau*, February 20, 1963.)

In glorifying the predatory campaigns of German imperialism the West German population is again served with a distorted description of the historical role of colonialism.

As of old, the ideologists of West German neo-colonialism allege that:

- Europeans had built railways and factories,
- misery and disease among the oppressed native population had been removed by the "whites."

The atrocities of the German mercenaries are being ignored or presented as humane acts.

The West German schools popularize this racism. Even as children, citizens absorb neo-colonialist ideas. They are taught about Africa:

> European settlers opened up that continent agriculturally, built railways, roads and bridges. They opened up mines and factories. European missionaries tamed the savageness of the Negroes.

(Erdkunde, textbook, Part II for the 7th and 8th grades, Progel-Verlag, Munich, 2nd edition 1959, pp. 83–84.)

If there are any lingering doubts that racism is not the official policy of the Bonn Government, then read from this West German textbook.

The Population

The Negroes: The original population of South Africa is the Bushmen, who formerly were scattered over the whole of South Africa. Today they have been pushed back into the Kalahari Desert. They are skinny, dwarf-like figures about 5 feet tall. The light-brown skin is like tanned leather. The nose is broad, the forehead short, the mouth has the form of a snout. They speak in a peculiar way, smacking their tongues.

. . . Each gets his job for the day from the chief. The women fetch water, wood and collect fruit. The men accompany the chief. Walking quickly, almost running, they slide along in a waddling manner . . . After their return the camp becomes restless . . . The harvest of the day is shown: roots, tubers, fruit, caterpillars, frogs, turtles, grasshoppers, even snakes and lizards. The loot is distributed and the meal prepared. Soon it is ready. Chewing with a smacking noise, licking their fingers like apes, they sit around the fire and greedily gulp down enormous quantities.

Africa–The Raw Material Base of Europe

During the past decades, the European states have carried out gigantic colonialization work in Africa. They set up cattle farms and plantations, built roads and railways, created shipping and airlines. They enlarged ports, erected dams and power stations . . . The Europeans have transformed dry land and inundated areas into plantations. They opened up the rich mineral resources and built industries which give work to many Negroes. The whites combated the terrible diseases, built hospitals and schools and tried to improve the life of the Negroes in every way.

Since there is a great scarcity in raw materials and food in overpopulated Europe today, Africa is to become the future raw material and food base of Europe. All European peoples can contribute to achieving this aim.

(*Länder und Völker*, Ausgabe für Mittlere Schulen– Countries and Peoples–Edition for Middle Schools– p. 48.)

The population of the Federal Republic is fed with lies and false reports about the German colonial past, culminating in the allegation: "The German people can be justly proud of their colonization achievements." (*Lebendige Vergangenheit*, history textbook for secondary schools, Volume 5, Stuttgart, 1961, p. 460.)

As one of many examples of the deliberate falsification of history in connection with the conquest of the colonial countries, here is a report of the colonial conquest of East Africa by Carl Peters, ill-famed for his cruelties:

The servants took their muzzleloaders and fired as soon as the main village of Seghas had been reached. Chief Bamwalla came to meet the strangers. "Welcome, white man, to Usegha."

Peters:	"We have come to bring you friendship from the great people of the Waduchi (Germans) who live beyond the ocean, and are mightier and greater than all others."
Bamwalla:	"Do you want to help me against the slave drivers who set fire to my villages and kidnap my people?"
Peters:	"Where the flag of the Waduchi flies there are no longer slaves. We bring you justice and peace, Chief Bamwalla. Do you want friendship with us?"
Bamwalla:	"I want it. What am I to do, sir?"
Peters:	"The steppe is big, Bamwalla. It offers much room, white men will come and houses and villages will arise where now buffalos are grazing. You will accept the laws the whites give you so that peace may reign in the country."
Bamwalla:	"And no enemy will be allowed to attack us any more?"
Peters:	"No, I promise you that. Moreover, men will come to heal you of many of the diseases you suffer from."
Bamwalla:	"I want the Waduchi to become our patrons."

(*Lebendige Vergangenheit*, history textbook for secondary schools, Volume 5, Stuttgart, 9th edition, 1958, p. 45.)

Such textbooks frequently exist in West Germany in more than ten editions, with a total of 500,000 copies.

This method of falsifying history in the interests of West German neo-colonialism subsequently culminating in the view represented by the influential *Deutsche Zeitung mit Wirtschaftszeitung* maintaining that world opinion was anti-colonialist,

> ". . . but that it was colonialism that had brought the African continent order and stability for the first time.
>
> "Colonialism has put a stop to the slave trade, tribal wars, and ritual murder. Any civilization and education existing in Africa is a product of colonialism."
>
> (*Deutsche Zeitung mit Wirtschaftszeitung*, Cologne, July 19, 1960.)

This allegation is consolidated in the same insolent way by the racist thesis of the superiority of the "white race":

> The whites in Africa are the helpers and teachers, the fighters against epidemics and diseases among man and animals, the breeders and tenders of better stocks and plants, the protectors of forests and the soil, the scientists and technicians in all fields.
>
> (*Die weite Welt*, geography for secondary schools, Edition A, Volume 2, first half, "Afrika" by Wilhelm Groteluschen and Gerhard Siebels, Verlag Moritz Diesterweg, Frankfurt, (West) Berlin, Bonn 10th Edition, 1961, p. 67.)

The self-sacrificing struggle of the peoples of Africa, Asia and Latin America for their liberation from colonial and semi-colonial oppression through the imperialist powers is also slandered in the West German press, textbooks and radio.

Although official Bonn Government documents declare that the policy of the Federal Government toward the Asian and African countries fully respects the peoples' right to complete sovereignty, the facts prove the opposite.

The basic attitude of the West German Government Party toward the newly independent countries in Asia and Africa was expressed in the statement by the then Chairman of the CDU Bundestag group, von Brentano, who announced shortly before the 16th Session of the UN General Assembly: ". . . Many of the young nations are not yet politically mature enough to be able to make a decision in the spirit and on the basis of the Charter of the United Nations." (DPA, September 4, 1961.)

The ideologists of the West German neo-colonialism propagate this theory of the alleged inability and lack of political maturity of the people of the young states in many variations, such as, for instance, *Der Tagesspiegel*, West Berlin, February 1, 1964:

> "The frank words that were, however, unfortunately uttered too late by the overthrown Sultan of Zanzibar that the island had received its independence too soon also go for the other African countries, which are today afflicted with attacks of weakness, economic ruin, chaos and terror.
>
> "Events in the Congo have again revealed the serious situation that has developed in the newly independent African countries. It is comparable

to the situation of many young people in modern society who have developed quickly physically but who have mentally remained on a level which corresponds to their age."

The West German ideologists of neo-colonialism slander the struggle of the newly independent countries. Atrocity mongering and reports about crimes are used to belittle this struggle for freedom and independence.

Under headings such as "Hell is Loose in the Congo," "Black Mutineers Rape White Women," reports are given about the liberation struggle in the Congo.

> "Horror reigns in liberated Congo," they write. "There is no limit to the lawlessness of the 'Jeunesse,'" and "It is a fact that the savage hordes approach Leopoldville plundering, murdering and burning . . ."
>
> (*Neues Afrika*, Munich, December 1964.)

The Congolese patriots, who want to liberate their country from monopoly capital, are stigmatized as rebels

> "who have now butchered almost the whole of the Congolese elite in Stanleyville and numerous Europeans who have only given their best for the country . . ."
>
> (*Neues Afrika*, Munich, December 1964.)

They sneer at the training of the People's Army of the Congo.

"In the second and more important stage of training, magic weapons are distributed which are to protect the life of the Simba (name for the liberation fighters meaning lion). At the beginning there was only the 'water of the Mulele' which, sprinkled on the soldier, was to protect him from enemy bullets.

"Since this did not, however, have the expected effect it was replaced by the 'Great Lumumba Medicine.' The Mulele Water made anybody who had been sprinkled with it invulnerable, the Lumumba Medicine, however, guaranteed anyone under its protection resurrection on December 1st . . . The People's Army had a chief witch doctor, Mamma Fumu, who had at her disposal a large staff of assistants, so-called 'defense specialists.'"

(*Neues Afrika*, January 1965, pp. 17–18.)

The racial arrogance and contempt of the "master race" toward colored peoples is expressed in all of their reports.

Iwan Kirchner, member of the board of editors of *Bonner Rundschau*, writes about the Algerian liberation struggle: "With the covetousness went the unrealizable wishes of the semi-educated people who are still the majority." (*Bonner Rundschau*, March 29, 1961.)

The rising of colonial peoples, is defamed as a revolt of "ungrateful children." (*Länder und Völker, Erdkundliches Unterrichtswerk, Band 3, Atlantischer Ozean und Amerika*, Stuttgart, no date, p. 28.)

In neo-colonialist jargon, the Düsseldorf *Der Mittag* (Dec. 20, 1961) expresses itself even more clearly: "Even though the colonial masters have gained any amount of advantages from their overseas territories, the fact remains that had it not been for them, the colonial peoples would still be climbing palm trees and living on coconuts and bananas. That the teacher is cheated of his profit might be accepted because he has feathered his own nest before ... That he is thrown out like a criminal or scoundrel ... affects all of us, also the non-colonial Germans."

The West German press threatens all consistent liberation efforts as follows: "Without the white man most of the new African countries now belonging to the community of free nations and being member states of the United Nations would fall asunder. Africa is a black giant whose flesh is kept together by white bones, nerves and sinews." (*Deutsche Zeitung mit Wirtschaftszeitung*, Cologne, July 19, 1960.)

The ruling circles in the German Federal Republic are encouraging even the old colonial powers not to "watch inactively" the struggle of the African and Asian people for independence. They give every possible support to the armed attacks against the freedom struggle of these peoples.

The *Stuttgarter Zeitung* of February 21, 1964 writes: "It is impossible that small groups of mercenaries should be allowed to be the pacemakers of a chaos which the governments will then no longer be able to cope with. These governments may not be angels. They often misuse their power or enrich themselves but Britain and France are not obliged to look on inactively when in Africa, in the name of self-determination, democracy and freedom, chaos is established from which great dangers can develop for the West and particularly for Europe."

The West German mercenaries in Tshombé's service, the West German supplies to Portugal and Israel prove clearly enough Bonn's real attitude toward the peoples' national liberation struggle.

The West German neo-colonialists also abuse and insult the outstanding representatives of the African and Asian peoples who are leading their peoples in the struggle against colonial domination and for the complete independence of their countries.

The leaders of the national liberation struggle are described to the West German population as "gangsters and brigands" (*Deutsche Zeitung mit Wirtschaftszeitung*, Cologne, Jan. 21, 1964, Feb. 14, 1964,) who have come to power through "blood and violence." (*Stuttgarter Zeitung*, February 15, 1964.) The late U.A.R. President Nasser, former Ghanaian President Dr. Kwame Nkruhmah and other politicians, such as Jomo Kenyatta, Dr. Azikiwe and Archbishop Makarios are grossly insulted just as Patrice Lumumba was some years ago.

Contempt, arrogance and hatred are expressed in the innumerable articles and reports published in West Germany about the liberation struggle heroes of the peoples of Asia, Africa and Latin America, who in Bonn are called "political ropedancers," "Arab carpet dealers," "ambiguous characters," "African potentates" and the like.

Let us take the case of a former Nazi, Dr. Eugen

Gerstenmaier, for many years President of the West German Bundestag. Gerstenmaier actively supported fascist racial policy and implemented it. In "Kirche, Volk und Staat" (Church, Folk and State), published by him in 1937, the most vile fascist racial theories are propagated.

Gerstenmaier is still today a typical representative of the master race ideology. He doubts "that the Africans can develop their own culture ... compete with whites, and correspond to a sovereign state."

He does not grant Africans the ability "to liberate themselves from the compulsion to assimilate the political, economic, scientific and psychological conditions of the West." (*Afrika – heute, Yearbook of the German-Africa Society*, Cologne, 1960, p. 12.)

At the same time he tries to weaken the African's effort to gain independence: "The question can now be asked what the Basari in the mountains of Guinea or the Ashanti in Ghana would gain by exchanging their way of life with that of workers under civilization."

Gerstenmaier glorifies colonialism: "The epoch of colonialism was not merely an epoch of exploitation but above all an epoch of great colonizing, that is to say cultural deeds."

Another official for many years at a high level of government is Kai Uwe von Hassel, one-time Bonn Defense Minister. He was an advocate of Hitlerism. Hassel supervised, from 1935 to 1939, plantations of the DOAG colonial society in Tanganyika in which Hitler's foreign ministry had a 36 percent share; during the war he trained agents for terrorist actions in Africa, the Middle East and Asia; drafted the September 5, 1940 plan of the High Command and Foreign Ministry to reconquer Africa. In the Federal Republic Hassel was prominent in establishing the neo-colonialist German Society for Economic Co-operation and the Bonn German-Africa Society. As Bonn Defense Minister he was responsible for supporting other imperialists against the liberation movements in South Vietnam, Angola, and the Republic of the Congo; Bonn's arms to Israel and the military-atomic conspiracy with Verwoerd; an accelerated involvement of African states in NATO.

Former Bonn State Secretary and head of the office of the West German federal chancellor Dr. Hans Globke was a participant in the drafting of laws, decrees and commentaries which enabled the Nazis to strengthen their reign of terror, to realize their barbarous policy and to prepare aggression, intellectual author of the pogroms and mass murders of the Hitler regime, actively involved in carrying out criminal actions against the peoples whose territories were occupied by Nazi troops.

In the same racist manner Globke assisted in the "Aryan" conquest and occupation of Austria, Czechoslovakia, the Netherlands, Belgium, Luxembourg, Denmark and Norway. After 1945, Globke was one of the prominent Nazis who quickly regained high government positions in the Bonn state due to their great services to the expansion plans of German imperialism.

After the Wehrmacht overran France, Ministerial Counselor Globke drafted the "colonial blood law" in the Nazi Ministry of Interior. Under this law, all "racially inferior persons," including Africans, in the fascist-occupied areas of Europe were to be persecuted and exterminated.

On July 5, 1940 Globke was put in charge of the "conclusion of peace" with France by the infamous Reich Minister of the Interior Frick. The "colonial blood laws" were intended principally for this territory. This is revealed in a letter written on September 2, 1942 by the fascist Reich Minister of the Interior on the "colored problem" in connection with preparing the peace treaty with France.

"8. Colored problem. The seeping of colored blood into Europe cannot be tolerated in the future; to the extent that damage has already been done, it must be remedied as much as possible. The following requirements arise from this principle:

"a) The lasting settlement of colored people (Negroes, Madagascans, Indochinese, Mulattoes, etc.) in France must not be tolerated under any conditions. Colored workers may not be engaged in France unless the work is of very short duration. Colored troops must not be maintained in France. To the extent that colored people are resident in France, they must be removed within one year to the non-European colonial territories of France corresponding to their racial origin.

"b) Marriage and non-marital sexual relations between colored persons from France or the French colonies and Aryans of whatever nationality will be forbidden and punishable by law, both in France and in any French colonies left to France.

"c) Colored persons cannot be given French citizenship. Those who already have this citizenship will have it taken away if they are more than $1/4$ colored blood; in case of hybrids with Indochinese or related blood, exceptions may be made. The introduction of a sort of protective citizenship for colored persons remains possible."

CHAPTER 13

Bonn's Subversive Activities in Africa

The Bonn Government has played a leading role in seeking to reverse the trend in African countries for independence and economic sufficiency. The new West German state has had four administrations: Adenauer, Erhard, Kiesinger and Brandt.

The first three were coalition administrations dominated by the conservative right wing. Under this leadership, former Nazis were returned to power and neo-Nazi organizations were allowed to flourish, while Communist and left forces, generally, were suppressed. During this period most of the subversive acts in Africa were conceived.

In the general elections of 1969 there was a swing away from the right-wing Christian Democrats. A new more realistic coalition, composed of Social Democrats and Free Democrats headed by the Social-Democrat Willy Brandt, was put in power. During the election campaign promises were made by Brandt to reverse the reactionary policies and replace them with policies which would help promote world peace.

During its first two years of office the Brandt Government took some steps forward in Europe, concluding official agreements with the Soviet Union and Poland recognizing the validity of postwar frontiers in Europe. By early 1972 these treaties had, however, not yet been ratified by the West German Bundestag.

Nonetheless, the possibility of a thaw in the Cold War exists, because the positions taken in this regard are not born out of subjective reactions, but correspond to the existing realities on a world scale, as well as the pro-democratic and peace trends in West Germany. However, the struggle will be long and difficult.

The Brandt Government has already violated many election mandates. One was to ban the neo-Nazi forces. To this day, it has failed even to move in that direction.

A highlight of the continuing Adenauer and Kiesinger imperialist policy is the relationship of the Bonn Government to the African liberation forces. Pressure for change has not been as great in this area as in others and the policy of the previous administrations not only continues but has been escalated.

Though there has been a modification of West German government policy in Europe, a continuation of the reactionary African policy could, in time, have an adverse effect upon that positive development.

The continuing role of the Brandt Government in Africa is indicated by the disclosures of subversive activities in Guinea and by a continued policy of support to racist regimes in South Africa, the Portuguese-controlled colonies and Rhodesia. It is vitally necessary for peace-minded and freedom-loving people throughout the world to be aware of these facts. It is imperative that all democratic forces understand that "peace is indivisible." There can be no European security in the abstract. Security in Europe is related to security on every continent of this earth.

Thus, a basic component of the fight for peace is to

reverse the present reactionary-imperialist trends in West German policy, which threaten to wipe out gains made by the African people over the last 10 to 15 years. This policy not only supports racist regimes, but also seeks to overthrow progressive-led governments.

We shall discuss how this is taking place.

On January 29, 1971 Radio Conakry announced that the government of the Republic of Guinea would break its diplomatic links with the Federal Republic. A communique, issued by the presidential office, said this step was taken because Bonn participated in the aggression launched by the Portuguese colonialists in November 1970, and referred to a "network of subversion armed by West German exports in agreement with the F.R.G.'s embassy in Conakry." According to Reuter, President Sekou Touré again accused the Federal Republic of having a prominent role in the aggression of November 22, 1970. He said that Bonn's "development aid" for Guinea had been a mere farce as its only mission had been to promote the Federal Republic's imperialist ambitions by way of economic infiltration.

Here are more facts about these machinations.

Late in January 1971 the National Assembly of the Republic of Guinea transformed itself into a tribunal, sitting in judgment upon the persons involved in the attack of Portuguese mercenaries on the African republic. Conclusive evidence was provided by the West African government as to the subversive activities of the West German "advisers" in Guinea. Two West German citizens Hermann Seibold and Adolf Marx were sentenced to penal servitude for life. (Seibold committed suicide several days prior to the verdict.) The other West German "advisers" had been expelled from the country late in December 1970.

In the report published by the Politbureau of the Democratic Party of Guinea the following analysis is made of the conspiracy plotted at the instigation of the West Germans.

The report shows the complicity of West German agencies in the attempt to neo-colonize the independent Republic of Guinea.

After the armed Portuguese aggression messages of greeting and sympathy were received from five continents. This included all countries maintaining diplomatic relations with the Republic of Guinea. The West German government was the only exception.

Apart from this silence there are two other revealing facts: the death of Count Thiessenhausen, director of the "Fritz Werner" company of Guinea, and the suicide of the F.R.G.'s ambassador in Lisbon. Count Thiessenhausen was killed by his Portuguese accomplices at the very moment when he fulfilled his mission to give operational support to enemy troops during their landing in the area of a strategic point.

The Guinean government has a photostat of an official document confirming the circumstances accompanying the death of Thiessenhausen as well as the psychological drama leading to the suicide of the West German ambassador in Lisbon. This document unequivocally proves the conscious and active participation of the West German government in the aggression against Guinea.

The secret West German document, found on Hermann Seibold when he was arrested, and later published by Guinean authorities is as follows:

"The Portuguese government's official attitude was orally explained to Ambassador Hans-Heinrich Schmidt-Horix in the morning of 23 November 1970. The Portuguese government considers that the events in Conakry are due to the existence of the PAIGC headquarters in that town, initial point of the principal attacks launched against the territory and the citizens of Guinea-Bissao.

"The government has a special stake in the destruction of this permanent hotbed of aggression and supports the fighting forces to the best of its abilities.

"The Portuguese government referred to a series of facts published beforehand on the strength of which any participation in the events is to be denied, officially. It hopes that this attitude will be treated confidentially and respected.

"The Portuguese government vividly regrets that the scheme has failed. Unfortunately, the oppositional forces in Guinea did not recognize that the moment had come to overthrow the regime so that a coordination of the activities could not be effected.

"Portugal pays tribute to Count von Thiessenhausen who gave his life for the cause of freedom.

"Taking into account the Africans' mentality, the

F.R.G.'s involvement with the events will become known. And whoever knows the attitude of certain African presidents and heads of government is perfectly aware of the situation, all the more so as it will be revealed that the arms used in Conakry are of West German origin. According to Portuguese statements this possibility cannot be excluded.

"If it is impossible to conceal the supply of arms from the F.R.G. to Portugal within the framework of our commitments in the Atlantic alliance, the German interest commands at least that Portugal's involvement in the events in the Republic of Guinea be publicly denied.

"In any case it can be foreseen that the relations between the F.R.G. and the Republic of Guinea will be frozen for a certain period of time. The circumstances accompanying the killing of Count von Thiessenhausen will be interpreted by the Guinean politicians as illegal acts committed by the representatives of the Federal Republic, as the leaders of Guinea are still largely guided by emotions. But now as before the F.R.G. will be able to rely on the aid and support of very influential friends in the government and in the ruling party."

The Politbureau of the Democratic Party of Guinea declared that this document did not require comment. About Hermann Seibold, it said:

"Hermann Seibold, director of the vocational training center at Kankan, was arrested on

16 December 1970 . . . After having been transferred to Conakry, Seibold was cited to appear before a commission appointed by the Supreme Command Council. The first search of his house yielded a large amount of incriminatory evidence, which induced the Guinean government to take him into custody.

"Four documents leave no doubt about Seibold's active participation in the events of 22 November 1970 and clearly prove the collaboration of Seibold and the Portuguese invaders. These four documents have convinced the Supreme Command Council that a secret West German organization was operating on Guinean soil with Seibold as one of its leaders. The investigating commission therefore effected another systematic search of the Bordo center at the instruction of the Supreme Command Council. As was expected, this second search brought to light a wealth of documents and papers which fully reveal the true aims of the Bordo vocational training center and the real role of the so-called German teachers employed there."

The report of the Politbureau of the Democratic Party of Guinea dealt in details with Seibold's record and arrived at the following conclusions:

"Hermann Seibold, posing as director of the *Centre artisanal* of Bordo, is none other than Bruno Freitag. An old, experienced collaborator of the fascist secret service, Bruno Freitag joined the Nazi movement at a very early date. Registered as a member of the NSDAP under no. 308,477, he was also in the Nazi party's shock troops, the SS, where he was listed as no. 380,352. "Bruno Freitag alias Seibold was also a member of the SS organization "Lebensborn" charged with maintaining the alleged purity of German blood according to the principle that the Nordic Aryan race was the most valuable of all races.

"Between 1937 and 1945 Seibold advanced to an SS rank equivalent to that of a major in the army. At the same time he worked for the Gestapo and held a number of posts in the Main Reich Security Office (RSHA) in Berlin. He was a specialist for activities of the Fifth Column in countries in which Nazi Germany was particularly interested, for activities destined to facilitate open aggression and the subordination of these countries to the Nazi rulers. What is more, in 1938 Seibold took part in the occupation of Czechoslovakia. He further distinguished himself during the systematic suppression of the antifascist movements in Belgium, the Netherlands and Norway. Bruno Freitag is also known for his activities against the French Resistance. After the war, Seibold worked on the Catholic Relief Organization in a number of "young people's villages." The head of this organization (Arnold Dannemann) is now on the payroll of the West German secret service."

Following his arrest, Hermann Seibold submitted to the Guinean authorities a list of his accomplices including the West German "expert" Adolf Marx, technical director of the Sobragui brewery. According to the report of the Democratic Party of Guinea (PDG), the interrogation of Marx led to the unveiling of particularly dangerous action groups involved either in shady currency transactions or in the bribery of political officials and civil servants and engaged in the military preparation of specially trained people who were to serve as a strategic auxiliary force in the case of an aggression from abroad.

Seibold's list led to more arrests, not only in Kankan, but also in Conakry, Dabola, Kissidougou and Mamou. The PDG states on this point:

> "The investigations showed that the espionage centres of Conakry pursued their activities with the utmost cynicism and had a very broad structure comparable to that of Bordo ... The West German experts in general, and—needless to say— the whole of the ambassadorial staff including the West German ambassador in Conakry, were active members of this network."

Adolf Marx's notebook showed that between June and November 1970, 20.8 million Guinean francs had been spent for the purpose of bribery. The Guinean director of the Sily-Film company received an Opel car as a "gift" from West Germany; two of his collaborators were presented with a Volkswagen each, while another who was also on the secret service payroll, was given a car of the Mercedes type along with a cash loan of 200,000 francs. A goldsmith in Kankan also received a Volkswagen. Cross-examined by the investigating commission, Adolf Marx declared he had received instructions for industrial sabotage from Count Thiessenhausen, the director of the West German "Fritz Werner" company. Additional documents and other evidence found in the West German training center of Kankan-Bordo included order forms for arms supplies from the F.R.G., notes on arms transports by special planes of the West German air force, vouchers proving the opening of accounts in the F.R.G. on behalf of Guinean agents and cash transfers for such persons as well as for the payment of weapons. In Seibold's apartment the police discovered three telescopic-sight rifles, two double-barrel guns, four reserve telescopes and 12,760 rounds of ammunition. Adolf Marx also owned a pistol provided with a silencer. A total of 151 telescopic sight rifles and 21 automatic pistols were found with the "advisers" and confiscated. As Marx stated in evidence before the commission, two West German nationals had been charged with leading the Portuguese commandos to the explosives dump at Camp Alpha Yaya.

The French news agency AFP, quoting official reports from Conakry, announced on January 27, 1971 that packages allegedly containing food had been confiscated, which were mailed in Hamburg and addressed to West German advisers. Arms and ammunition had been found hidden among the food. Quantities of weapons and munitions were distributed in Guinea through mail from West Germany since 1968.

Arms were stocked in the West German embassy in Conakry; ammunition was smuggled to Guinea in the drums of washing machines; planes of the West German air force were used for illegal transports of weapons and munitions, etc.

There have been Bonn government intrigues against other African nations in addition to the abortive invasion of Guinea. These have substantiated West German imperialist policy against the African peoples.

The session of the Council of Ministers of the Organization for African Unity (O.A.U.) held in Addis Ababa in September 1970 and the Conference in Lusaka vigorously condemned the military and international aid granted by the NATO states (including the F.R.G., Portugal and South Africa) and the close co-operation of Bonn and Pretoria as a serious menace to the security and sovereignty of the African states.

World imperialism has made use of the South African apartheid regime (also illegally occupying Namibia), of the white minority regime in Rhodesia, and of the Portuguese colonies, Angola and Mozambique, as bases and starting points for the implementation of its neo-colonialist schemes against the independent African states. This explains why imperialist elements in the U.S.A., Britain and West Germany have a special interest in southern Africa. West German imperialism has specific stakes in this part of the continent. Large quantities of uranium ore are shipped from South Africa to the Federal Republic. The F.R.G. takes an active part in the prospecting for new deposits. The West German firm, Kloeckner and Co., has acquired the absolute majority of shares in the South West African Lithium Mines Ltd. The Frankfurt Uranium company asked the F.R.G. government to provide surety for the prospecting of the Namibian uranium ore deposits, the largest outside the Socialist world, in cooperation with the British Rio Tinto Zinc Corporation. Prof. Hans Leussink, minister for scientific affairs in the Brandt Government, allocated subsidies amounting to 6 million marks for exploration work by West German uranium specialists in Namibia. In doing so the Bonn Government violated the resolution passed by the UN Security Council on the Namibia question calling on all states to "abstain from anything that may consolidate the position of the Republic of South Africa in South West Africa politically and economically."

A 1966 resolution of the UN General Assembly transferred competence for Namibia to the United Nations. This did not prevent Pretoria from refusing to comply with the resolutions of the UN General Assembly and the Security Council. The UN resolution of June 1970 called upon all states to suspend all business transactions in Namibia; to deny loans, credit surety bonds or other forms of financial support, destined to facilitate business or trade with Namibia; and to suspend all further investment activities including concessions in Namibia.

By cooperating with West German monopolies and with the Pretoria government in the exploitation of the mineral resources of Namibia, the government of the F.R.G. obviously contravenes the resolutions of the United Nations and appears as the enemy of the Namibian people in their struggle against the oppression imposed by the apartheid regime in South Africa. The ever closer economic cooperation (the F.R.G. is among South African's leading trade partners) has been accompanied for many years now by ever closer links in the military field. This collaboration is based on the still valid secret agreement concluded between Bonn and Pretoria in July 1961. Under this agreement, officers, scientists and technicians from the two countries are working together to develop and test missiles, to construct nuclear weapons and to produce poison gas. At the same time, Bonn directly supplies South Africa with arms employed to oppress the African population at home and to fight the national liberation movements. In recent times the Vereinigte Flugtechnische Werke (VFW) Bremen and the Hamburg Flugzeugbau GmbH as well as two French companies delivered troop-carrying aircraft of the "Transall C-160" type to South Africa. This is another flagrant violation of the arms embargo imposed on Pretoria by the United Nations.

Besides the South African racists, Portugal has been a privileged partner of the West German imperialists for the past few years. According to the journal *Wehrdienst* published in Bonn, the F.R.G. has provided Lisbon with weapons and military equipment worth about two hundred million marks to suppress the national liberation movements in Angola and Mozambique. This figure does not include the three 1,365 ton corvettes constructed by the Blohm und Voss AG shipyards in Hamburg for Portugal's navy. The first of these vessels, baptized *Joao Coutinho* was handed over in February 1970, the second, *Jacinto Candido* on June 16, 1970 and the third, *General Pereira d'Eca* in September. The warships are equipped with two 76 mm. guns, two 40 mm. anti-aircraft guns, two 40 mm. anti-aircraft guns, a "Hedgehog" type cannon and two depth-charge launchers.

In the course of the past few years the Bundeswehr supplied the following equipment to Portugal: 40 tactical aircraft of the Fiat G 91 type, special aircraft for short runways, 110 planes of the Dornier Do-27 type provided with 37 mm. rockets, 8 transport planes of the Nord 2502 Noratlas type, 60 F-86 K Sabre jet fighters, 111 Fouga-Magister aircraft, 10 Saro Skeeters (helicopters), and unknown number of tanks (M-41 and M-47) as well as pieces of artillery, heavy-duty transport vehicles, licences for G-3 rifles etc. (according to information in *Frankfurter Allgemeine Zeitung, Weltwoche, Die Zeit*, UN records etc.)

As early as June 1961 the Angolan liberation front MPLA proved that Bonn had delivered 10,000 submachine guns to the colonialist regime in Lisbon. What is more, West German officers are acting as instructors and advisers in the Portuguese colonial army. The cooperation in the military field is illustrated by the fact that the Federal Ministry of Defense has so far invested more than 200 million marks in the Beja airbase located southeast of Lisbon. The Bonn Government's military commitments are intended to safeguard the interests of the country's monopolies in the African countries under Portuguese domination. With a trade exchange figure of about 1,000 million marks West Germany is Portugal's number one trade partner. The Düsseldorf paper *Handelsblatt* wrote in July 1970: "In the year 1969 the Federal Republic came first in terms of individual projects and of the total value of investments and collective investments in Portugal with 23 and 24 percent respectively." Such is the nature of the relation of Bonn with the Portuguese colonialist regime.

The foregoing should suffice to show that the betrayal of the Potsdam Agreement by the Allied Powers has sown the seeds for another world conflagration, for a renewal of genocidal treatment of people considered to be part of an inferior race.

A contrast between the roles of the two German states in the struggle against or for racism also demonstrates that racism is not hereditary, but is a by-product of a bad environment. If you change the environment, then you get one result. If you fail to do so things remain the same.

In this connection, the basic difference is the environment capitalism engenders and the type created by socialism. Thus, the final solution to free the world from racist ideology and from imperialist wars is to build a socialist society. But even short of socialism, advanced progressive-minded people can make substantial progress against racist poison and imperialism. A good example is the growing differences between the people in West Germany and the ruling circles.

CHAPTER 14

The Struggle Against Racism, for Peace and Democracy in West Germany

The working class and the people of the Federal Republic of Germany came into the post-World War II years with the same desires and aspirations which characterized the people of the German Democratic Republic. They, too, wanted to build a society which would eliminate the war-making potential of Germany. This was expressed from the beginning of postwar developments.

The plebiscites and constitutional provisions and the programs of most political parties calling for the nationalization of basic industries meant eliminating the big monopolies and was a potent expression of their sentiments. The removal of the monopolies would be like removing the heart from the body of the war-making machine.

However, due to the betrayal of the Potsdam Agreement by the allies, the people of the F.R.G. were unable to realize their aspirations, as in the G.D.R.

Nonetheless, the people in the F.R.G., during the last twenty-five years, have waged magnificent struggles against all aspects of war preparations, encroachments on democratic liberties, racism and for better living conditions. They promise a good base to thwart the war and racist aims of world imperialism.

From the beginning of the rebuilding of the West German army, there was massive resistance, which still continues. At a crucial moment in that struggle, when Minister of Defense Strauss proposed nuclear weapons for the army and an increase in army personnel (as revealed in *Der Spiegel*), there was a tremendous wave of indignation and protest.

The changes in government personnel, the resignation of Strauss following the *Spiegel* affair, the commitment of Adenauer not to seek public office when his term expired, the necessity for Adenauer's successor, Kiesinger, to camouflage the war program and aims of the big monopolies, and, finally, the defeat of the CDU in 1969—all add up to a significant growth of democratic forces in the F.R.G.

The initiative taken by the Coalition Government headed by the Social-Democrat Willy Brandt to conclude peace treaties with the U.S.S.R. and Poland was in direct response to the pressure of the electorate in the 1969 election campaign, which called for an easing of international tensions in Europe and in the world.

Thus, the people of West Germany are an important component of the world-wide democratic process. They have been influenced by world trends, especially in the decade of the 'sixties. They have been influenced by the U.S. conduct of the Vietnam War, racial terror and internal issues, such as the Emergency Laws, political and social manipulations, difficulties in education and the revival of nationalism and neo-Nazism. These issues have had great effects, particularly upon the youth who today strive for more or less radical changes.

Disillusionment with imperialism was strongly influenced in the F.R.G. by U.S. policy. As a result, progressive students and young intellectuals sympathized with the national liberation and civil rights movement, which were expressed by the adoption of many of the methods, symbols and hues of these organizations.

In 1967 to 1968, the democratic forces in the F.R.G. became effective as an "extra-parliamentary opposition," which acted against the Vietnam War, the Emergency Laws media manipulation and nuclear arms, and for improving education and recognizing postwar frontiers.

After 1968, conditions of struggle for the democratic forces changed and, to some extent, improved. On one hand, there were splits; on the other, there were the establishment in September 1968 of the German CP (DKP); in May 1968, of the Socialist German Workers Youth (SDAJ), and in February 1969, of the Association of Marxist Students (Spartakus). These resulted from the mass actions and provided better conditions of struggle. They also increased the influence of the Communists.

The growth of the latter made it possible for me to go there. In the summer of 1970, I took advantage of the opportunity to go to West Germany and observe first-hand how the youth and the people are responding to the war in Vietnam and racial injustice in the United States. I spoke at several meetings in Cologne, Düsseldorf and Frankfurt-am-Main. These were of both a public and private character. The public meetings were called to protest atrocities such as had occurred in My-Lai in Vietnam, and the persecution of the Black Panthers in the U.S.

I was especially inspired by the youth. They, too, like their counterparts in the G.D.R., showed a keen awareness of the situation in the U.S. and of their own responsibilities to wipe out such injustices. During this visit, I came into contact with Black G.I.'s stationed in West Germany.

Although I should not have been, I was shocked by the widespread discrimination and persecution against Black troops. I thought that some progress had been made, but unfortunately like most Americans, I was ignorant about these matters. The American press at that time carried little or nothing about the situation. I had to go to West Germany to find out from the West German press and people that, although Black troops constitute only 12 percent of the Occupation Forces, they constitute over 70 percent of those in the prisons. In one prison camp, Black soldiers had been fed rat poison.

But it was heartening to learn that the troops were fighting back and that some West Germans were standing at their side. Very little, if anything, is said about this angle.

After I returned to the United States and made known the situation of Black G.I.'s, the American press began to admit and publicize some of the cases. The most influential Black conservative organization sent an investigating team to the Federal Republic. But the main burden of its report was to absolve those at higher levels of responsibility and to blame the landlords in the F.R.G. for discrimination against Black troops. This one-sided presentation adds up to a whitewash of the real problems and their source.

Of course, discrimination by West German land-lords exists. But what these people failed to report is that the West German workers, youth, students and intellectuals stand on the side of the harassed G.I.'s. A good example is what occurred even before my arrival there. A number of Black G.I.'s wanted to hold a meeting to protest conditions. They were refused facilities on the Army Post. The Rector of a leading West German university came to their aid, opening the school to meet in. Over a thousand of the troops came and presented a petition calling for: ending the war in Vietnam, dismantling U.S. bases in Africa, and ending discrimination in the U.S. Army.

This event was hushed up in the United States. I was the first to reveal it to the American public. Some months later, the press began to give coverage to it.

Regarding internal affairs, I found a growing readiness for struggle by the working class and its trade unions. The metal and chemical workers, in particular, defended themselves stubbornly against the price increases and the increasing gap between monopoly profits and wages. The self-confidence of a considerable portion of the working class grew during the spontaneous strike struggles of 1969, during the big strikes in the fall of 1970 and in the chemical industry in 1971.

Characteristic of the main strikes of the past few years has been their factory origin. Because of the rank and file actions, the September 1969 strikes were not officially organized by the unions, which meant that strike pay was not provided, nor was the organizational apparatus of the unions available.

The determination of the workers and their discovery of new forms of struggle, such as factory occupation, greatly shocked the employers. The unions made efforts to overcome the tendency, which had become apparent in spontaneous strikes, toward a separation of the unions and the workers. Strikes in the chemical industry in the spring and summer of 1971 showed that the union leadership had learned to apply new forms of struggle tried out in recent conflicts. The tactic of "lack of employer-employee agreement," the organization of local strikes without previous strike ballots, and the rapid extension of strikes from one factory to another—all this upset the solidarity of the employers. For the first time there was open solidarity of doctors and teachers with striking workers.

The general lessons of the strikes are not affected by the fact that the union leadership, acting under pressure from the Federal Government which had been called in by the chemical monopoly, abandoned the full-scale use of trade union strength and concluded an agreement which was described in many circles as a bad compromise. However, the struggles of the past few years, particularly in metal and chemicals, confirmed that the strike had remained the decisive weapon of the workers in their struggle for social and political rights. At the same time, these struggles demonstrate the limits of the policy of integration pursued by the imperialist state, with the participation or under the leadership of Social-Democratic politicians. In particular, anti-Communism is becoming increasingly ineffective as a method of preventing social struggles and of splitting the working class.

The social basis of these struggles is slowly widening. The strike movement has been joined by engineers and technicians (for instance, airport personnel), office workers and even government workers. The big industrialists observe this with great concern. Doctor Georg Juraschek, representative of the Federal Association of German Employers Associations, has spoken of a "Red renaissance." In an article, he stated:

> "So-called unrest is becoming active in groups which one had hitherto believed were inclined to think and act realistically, as a result of their type of work—that is to say, among engineers and technicians."
> (*Der Arbeitgeber*, Cologne, No. 9, 1970.)

Unrest and readiness for struggle are also growing among apprentices and school children. There have been apprentices' congresses, the first strikes of apprentices, and mock trials directed against the trusts. Apprentices and school children demand a decisive improvement in their training, more money for education instead of armaments, changes in regulations governing admission to universities, and the banishment of anti-humanist material from the school books.

The "Red Spot" action has spread over the entire country. This action is directed against the increase in fares in public transport and tries to show a connection with the policy of armament.

For several years the actions calling for an end to U.S. aggression in South East Asia have played a great part in mobilizing young people. The escalation of this aggression has strengthened the front of the opponents of aggression. A meeting in Paulskirche in Frankfort on March 20, 1970 called for mobilizing all democratic and peace-loving forces. The resolution adopted there read:

> "In the F.R.G. we can decisively contribute to this mobilization if we can make it clear to the U.S.A. that the majority of West Germans condemn the war of the American Government and if, at the same time, the Government of the F.R.G. is forced to reject the U.S. policy in Vietnam."

Many actions for withdrawing U.S. troops from Indochina have been connected with demonstrations of solidarity with Angela Davis, with the American anti-war movement and with all peoples of the "Third World" fighting for their liberation from imperialist oppression. The "Initiative for International Vietnam Solidarity" has been important in helping launch a broad movement which has demonstrated its influence in the DGB (trade union federation), the Social-Democratic Party and the Free Democratic Party.

In recent years, the anti-draft movement has become a mass movement. A main reason has been the war in Indochina. In 1960, 5,439 persons refused military service (including 68 in the Bundeswehr). In 1970, this number had increased to 19,363 (including 3,184 in the Bundeswehr). In the first two months of 1971, those refusing service numbered almost double those in the same period in 1970.

For years, the democratic forces in the F.R.G. have pursued a decisive struggle against the great-power ideology expressed in revanchism, in the "Europe ideology," in the negation of political realities and in the effort for speedier re-armament, as expressed in the attempts made by the ultraconservative forces grouped around Franz Josef Strauss. The democratic forces call for a limitation of armaments, for a European peace order, for recognition of the G.D.R. in accordance with international law, and against nuclear arms for the Bundeswehr.

At the moment, the spotlight is taken by the struggle to ratify the treaties with the U.S.S.R. and Poland, for recognition of the G.D.R. in international law, and for holding a European security conference. Particularly in the trade unions, the call for limitation of arms is closely linked to the demand for more social security. In addition, there is the struggle against neo-Nazism and the tendency to right wing extremism and open force, which result from the conditions under state-monopoly capitalism. The criminal traditions of German imperialism are certainly still alive. A practical example is seen in the plan to introduce "preventive detention," which has certainly not been abandoned. The "Campaign for Democracy and Disarmament" described these plans as follows:

> "We regard this as a resumption of the practices of National Socialism and a preparation to reestablish so-called protective-detention camps." (*Deutsche Volkszeitung*, Düsseldorf, Jan. 31, 1969.)

In Citizens Initiative Committees, the opponents of Nazism from all sections of the people defend themselves against the growth of the neo-Nazi danger, exemplified in the existence of the National-Democratic Party, in the terrorist acts of "Aktion Widerstand" (Resistance Action) and in the deeds of the political leaders of revanchist groups and the Christian-Democratic Union.

These have been some of the latest developments in the Federal Republic.

I returned to the Federal Republic in the summer of 1971 and found that the struggles had greatly accelerated. On this trip I participated in a protest rally in Bremen against the frame-up of Angela Davis.

I had the opportunity to talk to the people via radio and the press. I was also able to converse with some former leaders of the youth movement of the Social-Democratic Party. I came away from these discussions with a feeling that the Brandt Government will face continuous pressure from its own followers to reverse the course pursued by the Adenauer and Kiesinger governments in the last twenty years. Its own procrastinations and maneuvers eventually will have to be changed; otherwise, the masses will seek other alternatives.

These observations were made in June 1971 after my visit to Bremen. Later I returned to the Federal Republic as a guest of the German Communist Party (DKP) to its second convention at Düsseldorf, from November 25 to 28, 1971.

The conclusions I had drawn that the Brandt Government would be under continuous pressure to carry out its election promises had already been confirmed.

A number of important developments took place shortly before I arrived. Among them was the pressure within the Social-Democratic Party at its convention, where the rank and file literally revolted against the domestic policy of the administration.

The struggle focussed around the problem of taxation. The delegates were dissatisfied with the tax program which made the workers bear the main burden of taxes. They called for a program to shift the main burden to the rich monopolies.

The upsurge in the Social-Democratic Party was a reflection of the general trend of radicalization in the trade unions and the working class.

I came into the country at a time when the auto industry was in the midst of a great strike. Over 500,000 workers were on strike or locked out by the employers. This was not just another strike. It reflected a new mood among the workers.

Lawrence Fellows, a reporter for the *International Herald Tribune* observed this new mood when he wrote in the November 26 issue:

> "The strike fever continued to spread, hastened by the widespread feeling among the German workers that they have shown too much restraint for too many years and that the 'economic miracle' that has made their employers look so opulent has not done as much for the undemanding working men who had made it possible."

The situation in the ranks of the workers was one of the main topics at the German Communist Party Convention. A large delegation of striking workers came to the convention and were given a tremendous ovation. Almost all speakers called for solidarity with the strikers. The Communists also advanced a comprehensive program to help meet the growing problems within the economy as they affect the workers.

The economic problems were tied in with all aspects of political life in the Federal Republic. As I listened to the discussion and read the material I felt that what is taking place in the Federal Republic is a reflection of a general situation in the whole capitalist world. It seemed to me that the conditions in the post-World War II years of general prosperity had reached a watershed and that the trend from now on would be downward.

In the F.R.G. production for war purposes and the rebuilding of the nation from wartime devastation had run its course. In these circumstances a sharpening of class battles is taking place. To meet the situation the German CP called for an increase in the purchasing power for the majority of the people through higher wages, salaries and social benefits.

In other words the workers must increasingly get a larger share of their production.

In regard to the problem of runaway plants or transference of production to places least affected by strike situations, a problem arising out of the multi-national character of many companies, the congress called for a federal law which would prohibit any plant from closing down until all the workers had received adequate job replacement. As to part-time work, they demanded that the workers would continue to be paid full wages. They also demanded that paid annual holidays be increased and the pension age lowered.

In order to stop the continuous devaluation of the purchasing power of wages and salaries the Communist Party called for a democratically controlled state price freeze. This proposal has nothing in common with the Nixon wage price freeze in the U.S. which in reality drains the pockets of the workers worse, because profits are left uncontrolled.

The German Communist Party also saw the interconnection between a war economy and social needs and services. It therefore called for an acceleration of the struggle for peace and détente in Europe. It stated that the most important and urgent problem is the speedy ratification of the treaties made by the Brandt Government with Moscow and Warsaw and the early convening of a European security conference.

Alongside these general peace aims the party proclaimed the necessity for an immediate program to delimit the budget for armaments. It proposed that the budget be reduced annually by 15 percent, until it is reduced by half, and that the man power of the Federal German army be reduced correspondingly.

The CP declared that the nation must stop producing offensive weapons. It demanded the dismantling of bases abroad, the stopping of support to racist regimes in Africa, the ending of stock-piling of atomic, chemical and bacteriological weapons, and the removal of atomic mines. Finally that the payments to the U.S.A., to balance the costs of stationing troops in the Federal Republic, be stopped and eventually all U.S. troops withdrawn.

By reducing the unproductive armaments expenditure, the congress saw the means to secure funds for social, communal and educational purposes.

Thus the CP saw the problem in its totality and called for intensification of the struggle against the causes of worsening conditions and not just against symptoms.

The government of Willy Brandt in addition to supporting the economic programs of big business, has defaulted on its election promises to curb the activities of new Nazi elements and is passive in the face of a renewed anti-Communist offensive.

In order to oppose the ratification of the Moscow and Warsaw treaties, Strauss, one of the leading reactionaries, made it very clear at a CSU party convention in Munich that his aim was not only to ban again the German Communist Party, but he listed five other major opponents of the old reactionary coalition of the CDU/CSU (the old reactionary bloc which under the leadership of Adenauer, Kiesinger and Strauss had revived Nazi aims of revanchism).

But these efforts to turn the Federal Republic back to the hysterical wave of anti-Communism that characterized the decade of the 'fifties, takes place at a time when the consciousness of the role and disastrous consequences of anti-Communism has greatly increased. In fact I was surprised to find what the response is among the people. Shortly before I arrived in Düsseldorf an appeal against anti-Communism was released by one thousand of some of the most influential people in the Federal Republic. It was a list that included a large number of people in the academic field. An appeal of this character and with such broad sponsorship is so rare that I present its entire content:

Reject Anti-Communism

Appeal to All Citizens Conscious of Their Responsibility

Full of worry that a new anti-Communist wave could undermine the initial endeavors for a policy of détente and retard a democratic development in the Federal Republic of Germany, we appeal to all citizens of our country who are conscious of their responsibility.

Under the leadership of F. J. Strauss and R. Barzel the Christian Democratic Union (CDU) and the Christian Social Union (CSU) developed, contrary to their initial Christian and democratic endeavors, into a rallying center for all reactionaries. They make use of the tool of anti-Communism in order to prevent the implementation of the treaties of Moscow and Warsaw and a European security system. F. J. Strauss and R. Barzel also want to revive the anti-Communism of the 1950s in order to thus block any small sign of social progress whatsoever.

The CDU and CSU deal blows at the German Communist Party (DKP), the Communists, and mean to deal blows at all Democrats, independent of whether their basic conviction is Christian, Liberal, Socialist or Social-Democratic. Strauss did not leave anybody in doubt about that. Besides the Social-Democratic Party (SPD) and the Free Democratic Party (FDP) he named as opponents to his policy at home: sections of the publicists in radio, press and television, the German Trade Union Federation (DGB) and the "left radical organizations." Anti-Communism is a call for struggle against democracy and détente. Democrats cannot accept this without contradiction. It is now necessary to stand up against anti-Communism—otherwise the political atmosphere will be poisoned, rational politics be replaced by emotions of hatred and the basis for a peaceful settlement with the Socialist states be destroyed.

Therefore, we address ourselves to all democrats of our country and call upon them to reject any anti-Communist demagogics whatsoever. It blocks the road to a peaceful and democratic future to our people. It is of no benefit to anybody whatever with the exception of those people who want no true peace and no true democracy.

In the face of a renewed pro-fascist offensive in the F.R.G., the Brandt Government, while taking some positive steps toward a peaceful détente in Europe, exhibits great weaknesses, as already discussed in the African policy, in domestic economic problems, anti-Communism and racism.

In regard to the latter, the racist policies in Bonn have many similiarities to those in the Hitlerian era.

Racism is not only directed against Jews, but continues to effect other European peoples and Black Americans. Today there are over two million workers in the Federal Republic living under slave-like conditions. These workers come from Turkey, Greece, Spain, Italy and other places. They are recruited into the hardest and dirtiest work. Their conditions in this respect are no different from that of Black people in the United States. While racist propaganda is not as open against them as against people of color, nonetheless they are the objects of most reprehensible forms of chauvinist expressions.

They are often referred to as "dirty people, criminals, lazy and uncultured." The inference is that they are not as good as Germans, "civilized men."

Their housing conditions are indescribable. They pay much higher rates for quarters than do Germans. It is reported that in many instances five foreign-born workers live in one room with two beds. They take turns at sleeping in a bed. When I heard about this I thought of a concentration camp I had visited and had seen how people were forced to sleep on top of each other.

Black American troops stationed in West Germany are likewise subjected to this racist heritage of the Nazi regime and continued by the present ruling circles.

These troops are discriminated against by both Americans and Germans.

During the congress of the German Communist Party in 1971, Kurt Bachmann, general secretary of the party, took time off from his job of supervising the work of the congress to discuss this matter with me. He said that the German CP was going to make the problem of Black G.I.'s one of its main concerns. In some areas, he informed me, German Communists had already been active in the fight to support the G.I.'s although it was insufficient.

He assured me the party will do all in its power to organize the solidarity of the people in the F.R.G. with the Black soldiers, in their struggle against racism and against both Americans and Germans who practise or advocate it.

I saw an example of this solidarity in the campaign they are waging to free Angela Davis. Her case was a major topic in the deliberations of the congress. When I addressed the congress bringing greetings from the CPUSA and mentioned the Angela Davis case, the congress as a whole arose and put on one of the most splendid acts of international solidarity I have ever witnessed. For about ten to fifteen minutes the congress chanted the slogan "Freiheit für Angela Davis!" (Freedom for Angela Davis).

German youth and children in the Federal Republic as in the G.D.R. stand in the forefront of this great campaign to free Angela Davis. A new generation of German youth who did not live in Hitler's time. Together with the working class and progressive intellectuals they give hope that the present course of the Federal Republic eventually will be changed and it will join with the German Democratic Republic in creating world-wide conditions for an end to racism, anti-Communism, for human survival.

CHAPTER 15

The German Experience and Today's World

The German experience through two world wars and the two German states which exist today contains profound lessons for the people of the world in general and the United States in particular. The events of the last quarter of a century show that the great majority of mankind, including many Germans, grasped the main lessons from the period of Nazi Germany. Nonetheless, there are many people, especially in the Western capitalist nations, who did not grasp the substance of what was involved in the twelve years of Hitler's rule. Consequently, almost three decades later, the world still faces the possibility of catastrophes of greater magnitude than World War II. Many people in the Western world have shown concern about what took place under German fascism. They joined with the rest of the world in producing the Potsdam Agreement. But notwithstanding this deep concern, they did not understand the fundamental causes which produced Nazi Germany and which could reappear under new forms.

At war's end some Americans went back to Germany to study what had happened. Many returned alarmed. But most still did not see the underlying causes of the betrayal of the Potsdam Agreement in the Western zone of Germany.

Milton Mayer, an American correspondent, went to

live in postwar Germany to study the German mind. He came back deeply disturbed and wrote:

> "I came back home a little afraid for my country, afraid of what it might want and get. I felt that it was not German man that I had met, but man. He happened to be in Germany under certain conditions. He might be here under certain conditions. He might under certain conditions be I."
> (Milton Mayer, *They Thought They Were Free*, University of Chicago Press, 1955, Foreword.)

What Mayer and most others who viewed the problem failed to see was that the conditions for what happened in Nazi Germany were also present in the United States over a long historical period. They did not understand that the events which transpired there had nothing to do with man in general but with capitalism and imperialism, in particular.

Of course, the confusion that still exists in respect to the Third Reich has been largely due to an ideological campaign that the ruling circles in the Western world have consistently carried out. It is therefore necessary that progressive-minded people endeavor to place the developments behind the Third Reich in their proper perspective and discuss what is new and different in today's world. Throughout this book I have endeavored to present an outline upon which such a discussion can take place. I believe that this is essential to removing the conditions that imperil the existence of all mankind.

There are a number of lessons to be drawn from the days of the Third Reich. But in the main, there are several basic facts. The main aspect of Hitler's program was not fascism per se. Fascism represented a method with which to achieve other goals. The weapons Hitler used were anti-Semitism, the concept of Germans as the master race, anti-Communism and bourgeois nationalism. These ideological concepts also were a means to an end. The goal that Hitler pursued was the creation of a condition in which the German monopolies, the German capitalists, would control the world. The main reason for such control was economic in character. In the first several years after Hitler came to power in Germany he succeeded in establishing control over the economies of most of the nations in Western Europe. And the German monopolies were able to use slave labor and rob the economies of all the countries which the Nazi armies conquered. Thus world domination for economic reasons was the pivot of the events that unfolded in the days of the Third Reich.

This fundamental fact has been obscured by most writers in the West. They have dealt with the nature of fascism as the dominant thing. Now fascism as a form of state rule is the most brutal form of state power ever conceived by man, and the atrocities committed under this system are what most of the world reacted to. Their reaction to the brutal, undemocratic character of fascism was positive. But in today's conditions, it is insufficient to see only fascist terror. The people must understand the springboard for it.

Because many people did not understand the nature of imperialism they were not prepared to comprehend the meaning of the events which followed World War II. They were unable to penetrate through the lies and the policies of the American-Anglo imperialists. This accounts for the fact that in the initial years following the defeat of Hitler there was very little reaction to the launching of the cold war by U.S. and British imperialism. This is why there was little or no reaction to the betrayal of the Potsdam Agreement by the Allied Powers. This is why there was little or no reaction to the rearming of Western Germany. Thus the first lesson to be drawn from the German experience is that the struggle for world domination was the key thing involved. And it flows from this fact that it was not only German imperialism that had aims toward world domination but also the American imperialists. British and French imperialism were on the defensive. They were part of the complex of world capitalist powers which in the last few centuries divided the world into spheres of influence with themselves as the dominant powers. They were struggling to keep their powers over the colonial peoples of Asia, Africa and Latin America.

U.S. imperialism—that is, the big monopolies of the United States—participated in World War II with the same aims that characterized Hitler and his fascist forces. They participated in World War II for the purpose of coming out of that war as the main power in the future.

Of course, there were many in the American political structure who were anti-fascist. The great majority of the American people were anti-fascist. But subsequent events show that it is not enough to be anti-fascist. It is also necessary to be anti-imperialist because under the aegis of imperialism the United States could pursue the same goals as Hitler and not be recognized as a force comparable to him in today's world. The policies of the big monopolies were no secret, as was indicated in another chapter. Speaking on behalf of big business, Virgil Jordan, an American banker, declared in substance that the next half of the twentieth century would be the American Century. And the policies of the American government for the last twenty-five years have been in the pursuit of that goal.

But it is obvious that the U.S. policy makers have not drawn the lessons from the defeat of Hitler. One of the prime things that characterized the defeat of the Third Reich was the fact that the world had developed to the point where it is no longer possible for exploitative societies to maintain their bloody rule over the majority of mankind.

If the relationship of forces was of such a nature that Hitler could not achieve his objectives, then the aftermath of that defeat should have sufficed to show both the people of the Western nations as well as the policy makers that such goals are no longer possible to attain.

This is due to the fact that out of World War II the Socialist sector of the world expanded from 280,000,000 people of the U.S.S.R. to a socialist community which now exists on five of the six continents of the earth and embraces over a billion people; one third of mankind. This factor, coupled with the successful struggles for independence by the peoples of the colonial and developing countries—in Asia, Africa, Latin America—embracing over a billion and a half people, has basically altered the relationship of forces in the world to such an extent that world domination by any single power, or combination of powers, for exploitative purposes is gone forever.

But the U.S. policy makers do not accept this conclusion and most people in Western countries have not understood this.

U.S. policy in the post-World War II world, as expressed through the Cold War, has had the objectives:

(1) to roll back the tidal wave toward socialism
(2) to defeat the efforts of the colonial and developing peoples to achieve real equality and
(3) to establish domination over the capitalist world.

These three point objectives have been the keystone of the U.S. policy for the last twenty-five years. But subsequent developments also point up the fact that these objectives are unachievable. In spite of U.S. imperialism's efforts the socialist world trend has grown.

The national liberation movements have delivered one defeat after another to U.S. imperialist ambitions. The latest defeat, one of which is of prime importance in destroying the whole policy, has been the events in Vietnam.

The third objective of U.S. imperialism—that is, domination of the capitalist world—was in large part achieved. But even this victory is now in the process of disintegration. The United States came into the post-war world by virtue of its non-involvement in the main centers of war, its tremendous industrial capacity and its command of resources with the ability to dominate the economies of the capitalist world including its allies.

In establishing hegemony over the economy of the capitalist world the United States achieved what British imperialism was unable to do when it ruled large sections of the world. For Britain, France and Holland and other capitalist countries only controlled the economy of colonies. The nature of this control is seen in terms of the total output of the various economic blocs. In 1970 U.S. total output was 980 billion dollars, whereas the Common Market bloc—West Germany, France, Italy, Belgium, Holland and Luxembourg—was a distant second with 475 billion dollars.

The United States now consumes one third of all the iron and steel and electric power and oil produced in the world. The United States today has one of every two automobiles, telephones and radios and two of every five TV sets in the world. With only 7 percent of the world's land area and 6 percent of its population, the United States has half as much productive power as all the rest of the world combined. This tremendous wealth has come about as a result of the ability of U.S. imperialism to control the home market, the richest in the world, to penetrate the economies of the major sectors of the capitalist world as well as colonial people. These developments have been enhanced by the rise of what is now commonly called multi-national corporations, that is, corporations in which ownership is shared by forces within the home country with forces in another country. The first multi-national monopolies evolved in Western Europe from companies such as the Royal Dutch Shell, Unilever & Phillips. However, after the Second World War and especially in the last decade the increased productive capacities made massive seizure of external markets an economic necessity, and U.S. capital fought for these markets from positions of strength. It was not difficult for the United States to establish its domination over the multi-national corporations.

Toward the end of 1969 the annual output of U.S. subsidiaries had grown to 200 million dollars and according to K. Phillips, President of the American Department of the International Chamber of Commerce, by 1972 it will reach an estimated amount of 275 million dollars.

As of 1958 the sales of the foreign branches of American monopolies exceeded U.S. export of commodities by 50 percent. The branches and subsidiaries of American corporations have become the principal challenge through which U.S. monopoly capital directly penetrates the economy of the capitalist world.

The main investors in the European economy are the three American giants: General Motors, Ford and General Electric. These three companies account for nearly 40 percent of all U.S. investments in France, F.R.G. and Britain. It is estimated that General Motors has assets greater than those of 110 countries in the world.

The development of the multi-national corporations has given to the monopolies powers that transcend national state boundaries. They can determine what to build, import and export. They can determine many of the essential features in the economic policies of the host countries. More often than not, the governments concerned can do little more than put on record the wishes of the American companies. Here are some examples:

Some time ago General Motors ruled that its Australian subsidiary should not export cars to Japan, leaving the Japanese market at the disposal of the General Motors plant in California. This decision put Australia in a position where it could not sell its only competitive car in Japan at a time when Japanese models were flooding the Australian market. Ford Motors, for its part, planned in 1966 to build an automobile plant in France, but, dissatisfied with the terms, broke off negotiations and decided to build it in Belgium. All subsequent offers of better terms by the French side were in vain and so was the visit by a special French representative to Detroit, the headquarters of Ford Motors. Ford refused to renew the talks. Equally futile were the efforts of the West German government to talk Ford out of its decision to stop the export to the United States of cars manufactured by its subsidiary in West Germany and export there instead cars made by its British branch. Thus, the multi-national corporations have become the principal instruments to further U.S. domination of the capitalist world, and greater progress has been made in this connection than in other areas.

But here, too, the situation has begun to deteriorate. Policies such as enumerated above, policies which aim at subordinating the activity of foreign subsidiaries to the interests of a single strategy are also leading to serious general economic and political consequences.

In recent years rivalries between firms in England, West Germany and Japan have become intensified and there are those who foresee that in the coming decades it is conceivable that U.S. monopolies will lose their domination even within the capitalist world. In the past decade Japan, the Soviet Union and the Common Market bloc all added to their productive power at a more rapid pace than the United States.

An article in *U.S. News and World Report*, December 7, 1970, states:

> "Look ahead and you will find that if recent growth rates persist the United States would fall to third place in the next 30–40 years. Japan would overtake the U.S. in the 1990's to become the Number One power and Russia would surpass this country early in the next century."

These projections may or may not be accurate, but one thing is clear: United States domination of the capitalist world, as it now exists, will come to an end.

Thus we see that the goal of world domination as well as the possibility of dominating the capitalist world is a dead end street. And this, therefore, is the prime lesson that the people of the United States and the Western powers must understand about the nature of today's world arising from the lessons of the Third Reich.

The ability of the United States monopolists to establish economic domination within the capitalist world and efforts to reverse trends toward freedom in other parts of the world comes also from their ability to mask their true aims and thereby deceive many of their own people. Hitler's thirst for world domination proceeded in the most open manner even though he too resorted to demagogy. He, too, tried to make it appear that German imperialism was on the defensive and not the offensive, but his actions were so loud and clear that his true intentions were easily discernable by most people—especially in relations to the transformation within the state apparatus. The establishment of the fascist dictatorship and the elimination of all democratic processes engendered a hatred for his regime that was world-wide. U.S. imperialism for many years was able to camouflage its drive for world domination largely because it did not have to transform entirely the state apparatus.

During these twenty-five years or more encroachment upon the democratic liberties of the people has followed a consistent pattern. What has emerged in our time as a new feature of the state, the development of state monopoly capitalism and, in the United States more particularly, the growth of what is called the military-industrial complex. The influence of this combination for many years was concealed from public view. It was not until 1960 at the close of the Eisenhower administration that the nation became aware of the sinister character of this combination of forces. Ironically it was President Eisenhower himself who warned the nation of the undue influence of the military-industrial combination.

Presidents come and presidents go. New Congresses are elected and, while the power structure based on the giant monopolies is unable to have its way on all problems, the basic drives of U.S. imperialism have remained in full force. However, in recent times, due to many defeats on a world scale and increasing opposition on the home front, the diabolical schemes of these sinister forces increasingly come to light and the opposition against them grows. Nevertheless, there still remains a danger that the fascist form of state could eventually take over the nation.

This remains, therefore, a danger and the whole world must be concerned about it. Such concern must be consistent with resistance to every act of U.S. aggression anywhere in the world. Such concern must also result in world-wide responses to every act of injustice inside the United States, for if America goes fascist, the possibility of a thermonuclear war looms upon the horizon with greater possibilities.

While the imperialist forces in the United States pursue a program of world domination with many concealed weapons, the ideologies they employ are no different from those of Hitler.

First and foremost is anti-Communism. It was under the banner of anti-Communism that Hitler destroyed over 55 million people. It was under the banner of anti-Communism that the Allied Powers allowed Hitler to rearm the German nation and prepare for World War II. It was under the banner of anti-Communism that the U.S. and Britain launched the Cold War and the hot wars. Anti-Communism, therefore, has proven to be a costly ideology. It has affected not only the victims, but has equally affected the perpetrators of this poisonous virus. In fact, in a certain sense, the perpetrators have suffered more than the victims.

Therefore, another lesson arising from the German experience is that the destruction of Communism is an impossible task. Thus, for those who indulge in such dreams, and for those who fail to penetrate the real nature of this ideology, there awaits a terrible price to be paid by all humanity. If one is to learn the lesson of the tragedy of Nazi Germany then one must also learn that anti-Communism as an ideology must be combatted in all forms in which it is manifested, and in all countries involved.

In the United States this is especially necessary. Here anti-Communism has been a most potent weapon to divide progressive forces.

Under the banner of purging the unions of Communists, the fighting capacity of the labor movement was weakened.

With anti-Communism as a weapon Black liberation forces have not realized their potential.

Even in the ranks of progressives there are those who wittingly or unwittingly attempt to purge known Communists from leadership in the people's organizations. In some cases where there is no purge policy, some seek to play down Communist participation. In this way they seek to appease the reactionary anti-Communist offensive.

The ability of American Communists to have equal participation in the struggles of the people, is a fundamental aspect of the anti-fascist struggle.

The Social Democrats in Germany sought the isolation of Communists. In the early days of the Weimar Republic, under the leadership of Social Democrats like Ebert, first president of the republic, Karl Liebknecht and Rosa Luxemburg were killed. Under his leadership Communists generally were hounded and persecuted. But even with this background and record Hitler did not spare the Social Democrats from his brand of persecution. They too died with Communists in the concentration camps.

Let those in the ranks of labor, the Black liberation movement, peace and democratic-minded forces learn the lesson of Germany. Either unite with Communists and present a common front of all anti-fascist, anti-imperialist forces, or be prepared to unite with them in concentration camps or in death.

The second ideological weapon used by German fascism and which is used by U.S. imperialism today, but in a different form, is racism. Under the façade of the German master race and the inferiority of all other peoples of all colors including the majority of the white people, Hitler waged the most destructive war in history. Racism was one of the most potent weapons in the arsenal of German fascism. Here, too, this poison has affected the perpetrators as much as the victims. Racism came into the world for the purpose of sustaining slavery and world domination of the major imperialist powers. In previous centuries it resulted in the slaughter and the subjugation of most of the races of mankind, especially peoples of color— non-white. But in this twentieth century racism extended into Europe and resulted in the greatest concentration of casualties of any period in all of man's history.

Therefore, the lessons from the German experience require that the peoples of the world understand the nature of racism as it affects each and every race in the world, their own direct relationship to this poison and the high cost of the bill it will eventually present to those who embrace and practice this ideology. Again, the failure to comprehend this basic truth can also lead to the destruction of today's world. But racism today does not manifest itself in the same way as during Hitler's time. It, too, is presented in a most subtle manner. And if the world is to learn the lesson of racism in the Third Reich, what is required today is to understand how it operates today and the tasks that are imposed upon us, the people. Racism during Hitler's time took the form of an open, direct attack upon peoples that were set aside for extermination. This led to the slaughter of a million Slavs. Hitler carried forward his racist theses using biological concepts that science had already proven to be false. Nonetheless, through *Mein Kampf* and other methods, many Germans were led to believe that they were biologically and inherently the superiors of all other peoples.

The racists of today, while still propagating such unscientific views, do not do it in the same way. The basic method today is indirect. In the name of *aiding* peoples who for centuries have been oppressed and persecuted as inferior peoples, imperialism seeks to fasten the rods of oppression upon the people again. This takes the form of what is commonly called "neocolonialism." With this as its weapon, U.S. and other imperialist powers continue to keep the underdeveloped nations of the world in a state of economic servitude. Thus another of the requirements to understand fully the lessons of the German experience, is for the people of the oppressing nations to realize that it is as important to challenge neo-colonialist policies in Asia, Africa and Latin America as it was to challenge direct control as it existed in former times.

Since the end of World War II, and more particularly since the beginning of the decade of the 1960's considerable progress has been made in the struggle against racist ideology. This has been especially noticeable in the United Nations. Beginning in 1949 the United Nations has carried out a number of actions which have contributed considerably to annihilating racist theories. The United Nations at its Sixth Session called upon one of its agencies, UNESCO, to consider the desirability of initiating and recommending the general adoption of a program to disseminate scientific facts designed to remove what is generally known as racial prejudice. Since 1950, at a number of sessions of both UNESCO and the United Nations, programs have been adopted which have aided considerably in enhancing the understanding of peoples of the world as to the high cost of racist ideology. In the foreword of a book published by the United Nations, *Race and Science*, it is stated:

> "Since the beginning of the nineteenth century, the racial problem has, unfortunately, been growing in importance. A bare thirty years ago, Europeans could still regard race prejudice as a phenomenon that only affected areas on the margin of civilisation or continents other than their own. They suffered a sudden and rude

awakening. The long-standing confusion between race and culture has produced fertile soil for the development of racism, at once a creed and an emotional attitude. The virulence with which this ideology has made its appearance in the present century is one of the strangest and most disturbing phenomena of the great revolution of our time."

It stated further:

"UNESCO must face the racist problem—'the great and terrible war which has now ended was a war made possible by the denial of the democratic principles of the dignity, equality and mutual respect of men, and by the propagation, in their place, through ignorance and prejudice, of the doctrine of the inequality of men and races.'"

The United Nations also set aside the year 1971 as a year to promote the struggle against racism. These developments show that progress has been made in the struggle against racism, but as yet, it is inadequate to cope with the problem of the present situation. The struggle against racism today goes forward on a higher level and thus requires a higher level of consciousness than in former times. Above all, what is required today is concrete knowledge of the main forces behind the drive to maintain racism in the world, and the self-interest that is involved in its elimination. It is in this respect that the whole world community as well as the people within the countries involved must evolve a program of common conduct to isolate and defeat the racist elements, no matter where they are found.

All of the imperialist powers that came into World War II were racist, not only German fascism, but the Allied Powers as well. All of them participated in the subjugation and persecution of peoples of color. Nonetheless, at that time a prerequisite for significantly challenging racist ideology required, first and foremost, the defeat of German fascism. It was the main purveyor of racism. Today the main purveyors of racism are to be found in a new axis stemming from Washington, Bonn and Pretoria. In this context, the main racist regimes are the United States and South Africa. Both of these countries not only maintain racist regimes within their own borders but have combined for the purpose of undoing the victories that were achieved in the past two decades in tle liberating movements, especially on the African continent.

During the decade of the 'sixties most African countries secured political independence. But in the southern part around the Portuguese colonies, South Africa and Rhodesia there still exists a powerful combination of forces which conducts subversive and counter-revolutionary activities on the African continent. Even though the number of countries involved is small in comparison with those which have secured independence, they are very dangerous. South Africa is the most industrialized society on the African continent, and it has at its disposal powerful means with which to undermine the independence of other countries. Therefore, the struggle against racism in the 1970's requires that South Africa become one of the prime targets of that struggle. It is not only counterrevolutionary in respect to the continent of Africa, but its Black majority lives under conditions that exist perhaps nowhere else in this world.

South Africa has long been known for its policies of segregation. But during the last twenty years or more, over 50 laws have been passed of a racist character. These laws have been characterized by some as the "South African Nuremberg laws." (The Nuremberg laws were anti-Semitic laws passed during the Third Reich.)

Among the laws which were passed was a law which considers sexual intercourse between people of the Black and white races to be an immoral act. It is estimated that between 1950 and 1960 over 6,000 people were convicted under this law.

The apartheid policy of South Africa is characterized by laws dealing with a whole number of questions, the pass laws, for example. Every Black African man, woman and child over the age of sixteen is required by law to carry a pass book. Black Africans refer to this book as "the badge of slavery." A Black African is not allowed to live or work in any area without permission. The pass lists identity, permitted place of residence, work and payment of taxes. Any Black African is liable to have his pass inspected by the police at any time, and if he is not carrying his pass on him he is arrested. Many of those arrested are sent to work without pay on the farm jails for white farmers. There have been thousands of cases where young Africans, sixteen or seventeen years of age, slipped out of the house without a pass, were arrested and sent to a farm jail. The parents are not notified by the police. Only when the child returns months later from the farm jails do the parents learn what happened to their child. The number of people who are arrested and sentenced under the pass laws is tremendous. During 1966 more than 850,000 Black Africans were prosecuted for apartheid offenses. In 1967 and 1968 the number went to 1,100,000. (Annual Reports of the Commissioner of South African Police, RP. 39/1967 and RP. 47/1969.)

Perhaps one of the worst features of the conditions of Blacks in South Africa is the fact that they do not possess any rights at all, including the right to vote. The situation in this regard is far worse than that which prevailed in the southern part of the United States following the Reconstruction Period.

In 1963 a detention law was passed which provided that any person whom a police officer suspects has committed or intends to commit sabotage or any offense—that is, plans to take part in a protest march, demonstration or leaflet distribution—may be detained in solitary confinement for successive periods of 90 days without trial. No court of law has the power to order the release of a detainee. Over a thousand persons were detained under this law. (*Johannesburg Star*, October 12, 1964 and *Survey of Race Relations in South Africa*.)

Blacks who have resisted the apartheid laws have been jailed and prosecuted and many of them died in detention. These include some of the most prominent people in the Black community.

271

The United States supports the South African regime. It is the second most important investor in South Africa. In 1966 its investments were valued at roughly 700 million dollars. According to the *South African Reserve Bank Quarterly Review*, December 1969, the investment had risen to 945 million dollars. Thus hundreds of millions of dollars in profits are made by the giant U.S. monopolies from the exploitation of the Black workers in South Africa. The following tables clearly demonstrate the profitability of investments in South Africa. They also show the United States government's and American companies' stake in maintaining the *status quo* in South Africa. In respect to direct investment earnings or profits in South Africa, between 1960 and 1968, in millions of dollars, the following figures reveal the continuous growth of such investments:

Year	$ million
1960	50
1961	61
1962	71
1963	82
1964	87
1965	101
1966	124
1967	128
1968	120

Source: *Survey of Current Business*,
United States Department of Commerce

In respect to the average rates of return on direct investments, South Africa has proven to be the most profitable vendor of U.S. imperialism. The rate of returns of South Africa relative to the total world is revealed in the following figures:

United States: Average Rates of Return
on Direct Investments Overseas 1960–1964
(percentages)

	South Africa	Total World
1960	17.5	10.9
1961	19.6	11.0
1962	19.9	11.4
1963	20.0	11.3
1964	18.6	11.4

These figures show why the United States supports the racist regimes of South Africa. Thus it is imperatively necessary for those who would draw the lessons of the German experience for today's world to make the destruction of this government a central target.

The United Nations, in proclaiming 1971 as a year of intensification of the struggle against racism, called for an economic blockade of the South African government.

Unfortunately this boycott has not yet assumed the proportions which are required.

The South African Congress of Trade Unions wrote a letter to the Black workers of the Polaroid Corporation of the United States who had taken the initiative to prevent products manufactured by the corporation from being used in the implementation of the policies of apartheid of the government of South Africa. It declared:

> "SACTU believes that an important lesson is to be drawn from the militant action taken by the thousand black workers at the Polaroid Corporation. They gave leadership and guidance to the very important role the workers of America can and must play in the struggle against racialism and racial discrimination in South Africa. The American workers can, through direct action against American companies investing in South Africa, participate directly in the destruction of a socio-political system that is fundamentally and essentially racist, brutal, and immoral and inimical to every decent and humane value worth mentioning.
>
> "The action of the Polaroid Revolutionary Workers' Movement is not only a guide to all American workers but to all workers in Great Britain, France, West Germany, Japan, Italy and Switzerland—countries with heavy investments in South Africa."

The intensification of the struggle against South Africa on a global scale also requires equal reactions to the racist policies of the United States government as it applies to Black, Brown and Red peoples. In respect to Blacks, due to international pressures, tremendous struggles waged by Black people themselves and supported by many white allies, some progress has been made in overcoming racial discrimination in some areas of American life. But such progress is of a token nature and does not fundamentally alter the unequal status of Black Americans. Moreover, these token gains have been used to camouflage the fact that in an economic sense the conditions of Black America have worsened, especially in respect to young Black Americans.

The policies of the United States government and the conditions imposed by the monopolists on Black people represent a policy of genocide. Thousands upon thousands of Black youth have been divorced from the productive forces and, as matters now stand, will never again be engaged in productive work. The development of automation, cybernation and technological changes in agriculture are the main conditions out of which the economic and social conditions of Black Americans are deteriorating. In order to meet the unwillingness of youth in the Black community to accept these conditions, the ruling class is carrying forward a program of repression comparable only to the days of Adolf Hitler in the Third Reich. Terror exists throughout the land. Blacks are imprisoned, denied all elementary rights and shot down in jails, as shown in San Quentin in the case of George Jackson, and in Attica in New York State in the Fall of 1971.

Black youth in the armed forces have had to bear the most intolerable conditions of discrimination and racism, and there, too, the answer of the ruling circles to their refusal to live under such conditions has resulted in thousands being thrown into jails. Whereas Black troops represent only 12 percent of the U.S. occupation forces in Europe, over 70 percent of those in stockades and military prisons are Black. It is estimated that 40 percent of the population in most Black communites throughout America are unemployed and bear the brunt of the growth of the deterioration in the economy in the country. The struggle against racism today likewise requires world-wide struggle against every manifestation of racist practices in the United States.

The world did not react to the persecution of the Jewish people in the early years of the Hitler regime for which an awful price was paid. In recent times, world reaction to injustice in the United States has progressed. The world-wide campaign to free Angela Davis is a very hopeful sign that what happened to the 6 million Jews slaughtered in Germany will not happen to the 30 million Blacks in the United States. But to achieve this goal much more must be done than at present.

The third ideological weapon used during the Hitlerian era was bourgeois nationalism. Bourgeois nationalism at one time had some progressive tendencies –especially as it related to the rise of modern nations. But bourgeois nationalism was a by-product of an exploitative system and, as an ideology, it was designed to protect the interests, not of the people in the nation, but the interests of the business community. "The bourgeoisie learned its nationalism in the struggle for its own market."

Under the banner of bourgeois nationalism the most predatory wars in history have been conducted. Bourgeois nationalism alongside racism constitutes one of the main pillars of a reactionary thrust in many countries. The nature of such nationalism was explained by the German historian Meinecke who wrote:

> "A supersensitive nationalism has become a very serious danger for all the peoples of Europe; because of it they are in danger of losing the feeling for human values. Nationalism, pushed to an extreme, just like sectarianism, destroys moral and even logical consciousness. Just and unjust, good and bad, true and false, lose their meaning; what men condemn as disgraceful and inhuman when done by others, they recommend in the same breath to their own people as something to be done to a foreign country."
>
> (Friedrich Meinecke, *The German Catastrophe*, Howard University Press, Boston, 1950, pp. 23, 24.)

Bourgeois nationalism of the character described by Meinecke not only existed in the Third Reich but also among the Allied Powers who fought against Hitler. It was the source of their capitulation to Hitler in the earlier stages and it was the basis of U.S. imperialism's emergence from World War II with the aim of world domination. Bourgeois nationalism therefore merges with racism and anti-Communism as ideologies that are incompatible with the further advancement of mankind. Moreover they constitute ideologies that, if not checked or defeated, threaten the survival of the world. The lesson of Germany is that bourgeois nationalism in this century is obsolete, impractical and unnecessary. Science and technology in the twentieth century, and especially in the last fifty years, have been constantly imposing upon all mankind the necessity to readjust the relations between nations, races and peoples. Science and technology have called for a new mode of society based upon the concept of internationalism.

The late Wendell Willkie during World War II took a trip around the world and he came back impressed by how science had brought the world together into one world. He wrote a book entitled, *One World*, which sold more than two million copies and was described as the most influential book published during World War II. He wrote:

> "I have traveled a total of 31,000 miles ... The extraordinary fact is that to cover this enormous distance we were in the air a total of only 160 hours ... There are no distant points in the world any longer. I learned by this trip that the ... millions of human beings of the Far East are as close to us as Los Angeles is to New York by the fastest trains. I cannot escape the conviction that in the future what concerns them must concern us ... Our thinking in the future must be worldwide."
>
> (Wendell Willkie, *One World*, Simon and Schuster, Inc., New York 1943, p. 188.)

Willkie's insight into the future was keen, especially coming from one who was among the top ruling circles of American finance capital. The kind of global thinking that he spoke about was also conditioned by what he considered to be incompatible with such internationalism. He wrote further:

"A true world outlook is incompatible with a foreign imperialism. It is equally incompatible with the kind of imperialism which can develop within any nation."

(Ibid. p. 188.)

But the world envisioned by Willkie did not come into existence from the capitalist world. The kind of world he envisioned came from sources that he did not see or understand, namely, that in today's world it is the Socialist community and the working class movement which generates the kind of internationalism that is required to reorganize man's relations to the new technology and science and the removal of contradictions therein.

David Bruce who wrote the introduction to *One World* understood the force which wrecked Willkie's conclusions. He wrote:

"Willkie's world 'one in integrity' was short lived after World War II. The International Organization about which he dreamed came into existence but the unified world of free and democratic peoples that was the foundation of the dreams disintegrated gradually as the forces of nationalism was resurrected over the earth."

(Ibid. Introduction.)

The nationalism that Bruce speaks of is very tenacious and the bourgeoisie spends billions of dollars to cultivate this spirit. It is not only reflected in the international struggles between the imperialist powers, it also asserts itself in its efforts to undermine the unity

279

of the socialist camp and the world national liberation forces.

Intervention into the Socialist camp is made possible whenever and wherever socialist or Communist forces lose one inch of their internationalist outlook. The system of socialism is incompatible with bourgeois nationalism. It was founded on the concept of proletarian internationalism.

As far back as 1848, Karl Marx declared the necessity for international working class unity when he wrote: "Workers of the world unite. You have nothing to lose but your chains." It is fashionable now for imperialist-minded people to support all varieties of socialism based on nationalism. Bourgeois nationalism was a by-product of capitalist society and proletarian internationalism is a by-product of socialist society. The seepage of bourgeois nationalism into socialism can have but one meaning, and that is the penetration of socialism by imperialist forces.

In the underdeveloped countries of the world where national development did not proceed as it did in Europe and elsewhere, many of the countries, nations and peoples, never having had the right of self-determination, have led struggles of a nationalist character for separation from the imperialists, for independence. Whenever and wherever such a development has taken place and has been directed against imperialists, Marxists-Leninists regard this form of nationalism as progressive. But even in this connection the point is being reached where it is necessary for the movement for national independence to move over to higher levels of cooperation based upon mutual internationalist outlooks. After independence, the continuation of bourgeois nationalist ambitions in the underdeveloped countries can only lead to a return of imperialist domination in other forms. The imperialist bourgeoisie spends billions of dollars in this area to promote conflict especially those between the underdeveloped countries and the Socialist community as well as internal suppression of Communist and Socialist forces. It is imperatively necessary that the people on the African continent now relate their struggle closer to that of the world-wide struggle against imperialism and capitalism and in closer alliance with the Socialist forces.

Finally, it is essential to move toward the unity of the working class throughout the world. The rise of conglomerates and multi-national corporations makes cooperation on a global scale a necessity as never before. The ruling circles through these multi-national corporations can move their plants around the world at will. They can go to those places where the standard of living has historically been lower and use production from these points to depress the standard of living of the workers in the more highly developed countries.

Some sections of the working class are conscious of this fact and that is why the World Federation of Trade Unions General Council met in Moscow in October, 1970 and issued an invitation to all other worldwide trade union organizations to a round table conference to express their views on how to arrive at agreements which would prevent the multi-national corporate interests from taking advantage of the divisions among the workers along national and other lines. In its appeal it declared:

> "Trade union divisions, clashes between organizations which claim to defend the interests of the same class, today seem like a relic of another age, incompatible with the needs of our time. These needs are becoming more urgent day by day because of the political, social and economic changes that have taken place in different countries and on a world scale.
>
> "The working class is growing, new sections of the population are entering into production, the numbers in the trade union movement are growing prodigiously, but because of international division this immense force is still operating in a fragmented way, wasting energies which, if pooled, could have perhaps a decisive influence in the development of the modern world."

Thus we have reached a point where the working class can no longer confine its activities along narrow nationalist lines.

The lessons of Nazi Germany call for intensifying the struggle against concepts of world domination. These lessons call for a renunciation of the anti-Communist campaigns, the abolition of narrow bourgeois nationalism and the substitution of internationalism. They call for the brotherhood of the oppressed people of the entire world. They call for an end to racism. This is the only way unity of oppressed peoples can be established.

In relation to the aforementioned problems that

have to be conquered, the major objective of all anti-imperialist pro-peace, democratic forces must be to defeat the ambitions of United States imperialism.

It is especially necessary for the democratic forces in the United States to draw the lessons from the German experience. These forces must learn the meaning of the unity of diverse forces as a prerequisite for victory over reaction. The German people could have prevented Hitler from coming to power if they had been able to unite their ranks, but since they did not grasp this simple truth in time, Hitler was able to use divisive ideological weapons such as racism, anti-Communism, bourgeois nationalism, etc.

A commentary arising out of this experience was provided by the Protestant minister, Pastor Martin Niemöller when he pointed out:

> "When Communists were jailed it was all right—
> We weren't Communist; when Jews were
> hounded, we didn't care, when the union leaders
> were arrested we preferred to keep quiet...
> When I was jailed it was too late."

We on the American scene have made great progress in the fight for world peace. The reaction of the nation to the war in Vietnam is a case in point. But notwithstanding this tremendous development, the forces of reaction on most issues are still able to divide the democratic-minded forces.

The main weapons, in this regard, are the same as those employed by Hitler, racism, anti-Communism and bourgeois nationalism. The fascist danger in the United States can finally be defeated only when a substantial majority of the American people reject these ideologies and struggle vigorously against them. What is required is that the Black "thing," the white "thing," the labor "thing" must all become the backbone of a broad peoples' "thing" that stands united at all times against the reactionary-pro-fascist-imperialist thrust. This is the main lesson of Germany.

In 1940 in the midst of World War II Thomas Mann, the noted German writer, addressed an appeal to the peoples of Germany over Radio BBC which was later published under the title of *Listen, Germany*.

In his appeal he warned the German people of what was to come. He stated:

> "What will become of the European continent, what of Germany itself, if the war lasts another three or four years is a question we all ask ourselves here, and one which the German nation ponders with horror. The present misery is only a mild indication of what must come . . ."
>
> (Thomas Mann, *Listen, Germany*, Alfred A. Knopf, New York 1943, p. 9.)

The German people did not listen. They followed Hitler from one disaster to another to the very end.

Like Thomas Mann I want to warn my people, the American people of a threatening catastrophe. I have traveled to Germany many times and I have studied the German experience, not only from books, but from the realities, and I have come away from these travels deeply disturbed about where we as a nation are heading. Listen, Mr. and Mrs. America! We have built in our land one of the most highly developed productive machines that the world has ever seen. We have created the instruments which could give a good life to every single American citizen and still have a lot left over with which to help our brothers and sisters around the world to achieve a comparable status. But because of narrow bourgeois interest, racism and anti-Communism these potentials are not only not being achieved but our nation is rotting away. It is common talk these days to refer to the U.S.A. as "the sick society." For amidst our affluence we have a country that is deteriorating both economically and morally.

Listen Mr. and Mrs. America! There is still time to save our nation from an impending catastrophe. The question is: Will we learn the lessons of Nazi Germany? Will we learn the lesson of the G.D.R.? I am certain that if 6 million Germans who died as the result of Hitler and his thirst for world domination could rise up out of their graves and speak to us they would say, "If only we had known what the end result would be, we would have followed a different course! We did not realize that when we exploited and killed others that we were digging our own graves."

Listen, Mr. and Mrs. America! We must not wait until it is too late! Our job is to do what has to be done before the fact. We cannot wait until the reactionary forces take power completely. The survival of the nation and the world will be at stake. And unlike the German people, we may not be able to rise up out of the depths of despair and build a G.D.R. I have confidence that the American people, both Black and white, will draw the lessons of Germany in time. My confidence is reinforced as I look upon a new generation of Americans, Black and white, who are picking up the torches for a better world. This generation is symbolized by a sixteen-year-old high school student, who calls upon America to:

Listen America

Listen America
You of revolution
You of fear and apathy
Listen to us
Listen to the masses
We no longer fear your money and arms
You of the armed command
There is strength in our young bodies
We are only beginning to flex these muscles
Listen you who control the media
The ones who tell nothing of the truth in mass struggles
It is twenty-five years since that bomb
That moment of death and destruction
We've come a long way
Now the fight is against the lies of the Pentagon
Listen America
Your revolutionary heritage is still alive
Don't deny it
We are alive and in the union is our strength
And there will be no Armageddon
Only Peace and Socialism
There will be no more Kents and Jacksons
No more Vietnams, Laos, Cambodias
No more Koreas
Hear our shouts and cries
See our strength

Listen America
Your sons and daughters hear your pleading cry
We heed the calls of the present and future
I live for the day my children will grow up free
Free of prejudice hate and exploitation
For the day of those "green pastures of plenty"
When none shall want and all shall have
No more polluting
No more "accidental" deaths
No more mangled workers
Yes America I can see a new day
I can see it coming
Judgement day for the capitalist is coming
No more "niggers" "injuns" "chinks" "honkies"
Pride in one's heritage and contributions to this nation
Yes America we are all one
United and militant
Listen America

Lynn Becchetti

Briefly,
ABOUT THE AUTHOR

A leading Black U.S. Communist, Claude Lightfoot has been involved in the struggles of the American people both Black and white for over forty years. During the thirties and forties he participated in anti-fascist activities at home and abroad, conferring with leading German anti-fascists. He was a delegate of the U.S. Communist Party at the Seventh World Congress of the Communist International (Moscow in 1935) where Dimitroff made his famous speech on how to defeat fascism. Thereafter, he participated in the Sixth World Congress of the Young Communist International where he was elected to the Executive Committee. In 1941 he volunteered in the U.S. Army. Since World War II he has held prominent posts in the CPUSA including National Vice Chairman. At present he is a member of the Political Bureau and head of the Department of Black Liberation. His Marxist analyses of the liberation movement have been widely circulated. A list of his published works is carried on page four of this volume.